LEADERSHIP THROUGH COLLABORATION:
ALTERNATIVES TO THE HIERARCHY

Michael Koehler
Jeanne C. Baxter

Routledge
Taylor & Francis Group
New York London

First Published 1997 by Eye On Education

Published 2013 by Routledge
711 Third Avenue, New York, NY, 10017, USA
2 Park Square, Milton Park, Abingdon, Oxon OX14 4RN

Routledge is an imprint of the Taylor & Francis Group, an informa business

Library of Congress Cataloging-in-Publication Data

Koehler, Mike, 1938-
    Leadership through collaboration : alternatives to the hierarchy /
Michael Koehler, Jeanne Baxter.
        p.   cm.
    Includes bibliographical references.
    ISBN 1-883001-30-7
    1. Teacher participation in administration--United States.
2. Educational leadership--United States. 3. Educational change-
-United States. 4. School management and organization--United
States. I. Baxter, Jeanne, 1934-   . II. Title.
LB2806.45.K64 1997
371.2'00973--dc20   96-31390
                                                              CIP

10 9 8 7 6 5 4 3 2 1

ISBN 978-1-883-001-30-8 (hbk)

Published by Eye On Education:

Block Scheduling: A Catalyst for Change in High Schools
by Robert Lynn Canady and Michael D. Rettig

Teaching in the Block: Strategies for Engaging Active Learners
edited by Robert Lynn Canady and Michael D. Rettig

Educational Technology: Best Practices from America's Schools
by William C. Bozeman and Donna J. Baumbach

The Educator's Brief Guide to Computers in the Schools
by Eugene F. Provenzano

Handbook of Educational Terms and Applications
by Arthur K. Ellis and Jeffrey T. Fouts

Research on Educational Innovations
by Arthur K. Ellis and Jeffrey T. Fouts

Research on School Restructuring
by Arthur K. Ellis and Jeffrey T. Fouts

Hands-on Leadership Tools for Principals
by Ray Calabrese, Gary Short, and Sally Zepeda

The Principal's Edge
by Jack McCall

The Administrator's Guide to School-Community Relations
by George E. Pawlas

Leadership: A Relevant and Realistic Role for Principals
by Gary M. Crow, L. Joseph Matthews, and Lloyd E. McCleary

**Organizational Oversight:
Planning and Scheduling for Effectiveness**
by David A. Erlandson, Peggy L. Stark, and Sharon M. Ward

Motivating Others: Creating the Conditions
by David P. Thompson

Oral and Noverbal Expression
by Ivan Muse

**The School Portfolio:
A Comprehensive Framework for School Improvement**
by Victoria L. Bernhardt

School-to-Work
by Arnold H. Packer and Marion W. Pines

Innovations in Parent and Family Involvement
by William Rioux and Nancy Berla

The Performance Assessment Handbook
Volume 1: Portfolios and Socratic Seminars
by Bil Johnson

The Performance Assessment Handbook
Volume 2: Performances and Exhibitions
by Bil Johnson

Bringing the NCTM Standards to Life
by Lisa B. Owen and Charles E. Lamb

Mathematics the Write Way
by Marilyn S. Neil

Transforming Education Through Total Quality
Management: A Practitioner's Guide
by Franklin P. Schargel

Quality and Education: Critical Linkages
by Betty L. McCormick

The Educator's Guide to Implementing Outcomes
by William J. Smith

Schools for All Learners: Beyond the Bell Curve
by Renfro C. Manning

TABLE OF CONTENTS

ABOUT THE AUTHORS viii
FOREWORD ix
THE 14 MYTHS THAT INFLUENCE THE ORGANIZATION
    AND CHARACTER OF SCHOOLS xi

1 TAKING A CLOSE LOOK AT EDUCATION'S HIERARCHY . . . 1
    The Origins of the Hierarchy 3
    The Paradox of Hierarchies 4
    Taking Another Look at Our Origins 6
    The Intransigence of Tradition 7
    The Need for Rationality 8
    Collaboration in its Broadest Sense 9
    The Rise of Collegiality 11
    Some Representative Programs 13
    Bass Elementary School 14
    References 21

2 THE HIERARCHY'S INVISIBLE ORGANIZATION 23
    Education's Invisible Organization 24
    What Are the Purposes of In-service
        Training Programs? 27
    Who Are the Clients of Our Schools? 28
    Change Is Not an Illusion 29
    The College School 33
    References 45

3 THE HIERARCHY AND TEACHER MOTIVATION 47
    The Farmer and the Seed: A Fable 48
    Motivation and Teachers 49
    Looking for Problems 51
    Self-reflection and the Hierarchy 54
    George Westinghouse
        Vocational High School 56
    References 62

4   DECENTRALIZING ADMINISTRATIVE DECISIONS 63
What are the Implications? 64
The Teacher as Codependent 67
The Search For Status and Teacher Burnout 68
The Contradiction of Caring 68
Old Habits Die Hard 69
The Inner Circle Syndrome 71
Who, Then, is the School's Instructional Leader? 71
Hawthorne Elementary School 73
References 82

**5   COLLABORATION AND THE PROFESSIONAL
GROWTH PROGRAM** 83
The Willingness to Change 84
    Five Questions That Characterize
        Teacher Observation 85
    Considering the Answers 85
Distinguishing Between Evaluation and Supervision .. 86
A Golf Analogy 87
The Need for a Shift of Focus 87
The Process is Simple 89
    A Quick Example 90
Theory-Based Practice 91
These Programs are Not for Everyone 92
Integrating In-Service Training Activities 93
When Collegiality Doesn't Work 95
    Program Number One 96
Deerfield High School 99
References 112

6   THE HIERARCHY AND PARENT INVOLVEMENT 113
What are the Responses from School Systems? 115
The Community Connection 117
The Principles of Synergy Revisited 118
Acknowledging and Accommodating
    Changing Needs 118
Where Does Such Proactive Planning Start? 119
Madison Middle School 2000 122

7 THE SCHOOL HIERARCHY AND THE STUDENT BODY ... 131
   Values Education and Religion 133
   What are These Values? 136
   The Realities of Student Discipline 136
   Taking a Look at External and Internal Discipline 139
   The Hierarchy and Student Behavior:
       The Big Picture 139
   Thompson Middle School 142

8 COLLABORATIVE INPUT INTO SCHOOL POLICY 149
   Theory Revisited 150
   Supervision as a Process 151
   Supervision Redefined 152
   Extending the Redefinition 153
   Increasing Synergy in Schools 154
   The Collaborative System 155
   Patience is the Key 156
   Pierce School 160
   References 171

9 EDUCATION'S HIERARCHY AND THE
   NEED FOR CHANGE 173
   Change Remains an Illusion 174
   Education's Natural Resistance to Change 175
   Change is Still Needed 175
   Change as Reactive or Proactive 177
   More About Trends and the Change Process 184
   The Elements of Collaborative Planning 185
   The Relationship of Hiring to Change 187
   Waggoner School 190

10 EDUCATION'S HIERARCHY: ITS LIKELY FUTURES 197
   Taking Another Look at Education's Trends 199
   What is the Future of Education's Hierarchy? 200
   Can it Happen? 202
   A New Awakening 204
   Taking a Look at the Current Literature 206
   The Most Likely Future 208

SELECTED BIBLIOGRAPHY 211

ABOUT THE AUTHORS

Mike Koehler, a former high school teacher, counselor, and supervisor, has been an adjunct professor of educational administration and supervision at Northeastern Illinois University since 1974. Currently, he is devoting all his time to writing, teaching at the university level, speaking at conventions, and consulting with schools on teacher supervision and on the eligibility and recruitment of student athletes. Mike is the author of scores of articles for professional journals, a nationally syndicated radio show, and a newspaper column.

Mike has written 12 books, including *The Department Head's Survival Guide* and *Advising Student Athletes Through the College Recruitment Process.* He is currently writing a book about his grandfather, Jim Thorpe.

Mike Koehler may be contacted by writing or calling Ideation, Inc., 8246 Voss Road, Minocqua, WI 54548, 715/358-8802.

Jeanne C. Baxter joined the faculty of Northeastern Illinois University of Chicago shortly after receiving her doctorate from Northwestern University in 1985. She has served as a teacher, principal, and assistant superintendent in the Illinois north shore districts of Winnetka and Glencoe. For the past decade, Jeanne has devoted much of her energy to Chicago's school reform efforts. As director of Project Co-Lead (Collaborative Leadership), she has been involved in the leadership development of Chicago's public school principals. She also directed a U.S. Department of Education grant to develop a model for urban principal development.

She is recognized for her workshops on leadership, managing change, and teambuilding, and is an associate of Quality Education Associates, a group that provides training and long-term support for quality improvement to school systems nationwide and internationally.

Jeanne C. Baxter may be reached at Northeastern Illinois University, 5500 N. St. Louis Avenue, Chicago, IL 60625, e-mail: Jbaxter@neiu.edu.

FOREWORD

Organizations everywhere are espousing the benefits of collaboration in the work setting. Whether represented by education, business, or one of the health industries, **we are in a turn-of-the-century era of change**, accompanied by a movement toward global involvement that requires teamwork. Corollary considerations inevitably involve shared decision-making, site-based management, participative and facilitative leadership, and (in education) teacher empowerment. The terms have been around for a long time, and they continue to echo through the halls of ivy and in and out of school systems across the country.

Practitioners, often in partnership with universities, look to the research and literature for guidance. Schools are encouraged to "empower" teachers, to share decisional authorities with them and to realize their increased commitment to organizational decisions. Such recommendations for collaboration have been reinforced over the decades and continue today. One has only to pick up the latest professional journal to find very convincing arguments for schools to engage teachers and administrators in collaborative planning and decision-making.

But collaboration has not always worked. Many schools, for example, have invested deeply in shared decision-making and site-based management only to find that teaching and learning have not changed. Some form of collaboration, it appears, can bring about structural changes, but not the deep cultural changes that alter basic assumptions and create new teaching practice. Too often, empowerment is viewed as a downhill stream with power flowing from administrators to teachers, somehow bathing them in decision-making authorities. Instead, empowerment needs to be viewed as a stream that alternately flows **both ways**, one day amplifying the authorities of teachers, the next increasing administration's sphere of influence within the building and the community.

This book considers both dimensions of empowerment and provides examples of how collaboration in schools results in increased power for everyone in the building and most important, success for the learner. It also takes a daring look at hierarchical interferences to such collaboration and suggests processes that make education's hierarchy more "user friendly."

As such, this is a book for practicing administrators, teachers, and university faculty who are helping facilitate change in our schools. It shares a powerful and at times entertaining message and is essential reading for anyone who wants to enhance the organizational effectiveness of schools in order to improve the quality of education for all students.

Thomas J. Sergiovanni
Lillian Radford Professor of Education
Trinity University
San Antonio, Texas

DEDICATION

The authors would like to dedicate this book to their immediate families for providing unqualified support of our efforts over the years to "spread the word" about changing patterns of educational leadership.

To the hundreds of students over the years who have accepted the challenge not only to master such concepts but to adopt the behaviors that bring them to life, we offer our sincere appreciation. Without their adaptability and sense of purpose, meaningful change in education's hierarchy is not possible.

Michael Koehler
Jeanne C. Baxter

THE 14 MYTHS THAT INFLUENCE THE ORGANIZATION AND CHARACTER OF SCHOOLS

Myth Number One: "The upper levels of the hierarchy are occupied by the most experienced and most knowledgable people in the school."

Myth Number Two: "Most schools operate and should be expected to operate in purely rational ways."

Myth Number Three: "Many school systems in this country range from most bureaucratic/hierarchial to most collaborative."

Myth Number Four: "Persons occupying positions in the hierarchy are not only organizationally superior to others in the building but are better than they are in many ways."

Myth Number Five: "Managerial incentives, control factors, and working conditions have primary influence on the professional behaviors of teachers."

Myth Number Six: "The growing number of 'burned out' or otherwise intransigent teachers in many of the nations' schools constitutes a serious challenge to school hierarchies to identify improved ways to influence teacher behavior."

Myth Number Seven: "The quantity and quality of the decisions one makes in an organization determine the degree of his or her power."

Myth Number Eight: "Well-conceived programs that provide frequent evaluation of teachers by members of the hierarchy are the best process for promoting continued professional growth."

Myth Number Nine: "Professional growth programs in many of the nation's schools, consisting traditionally of in-service training, supervision, and evaluation, reflect the responsibility of school hierarchies to provide carefully coordinated growth experiences for their teachers."

Myth Number Ten: "Education's hierarchy, recognizing the basic principles of systems theory, encourages its subsystems (generally the school's individual departments) to maintain a constant exchange of energy and resources with the parent community and other significant school populations."

Myth Number Eleven: "Being the primary clients of the school's program, students regularly receive opportunities from most school hierarchies to maintain or change curriculum and instruction."

Myth Number Twelve: "The hierarchy provides the policies and procedures that represent the primary authority for the control of student behavior."

Myth Number Thirteen: "Because hierarchical responsibilities promote a view of 'The Big Picture,' school administrators are the logical persons to make most, if not all, of the school's instructional and curricular planning decisions."

Myth Number Fourteen: "The hierarchy is the primary force that maintains the roles and responsibilities for accommodating the adaptive needs of the school."

1

TAKING A CLOSE LOOK AT EDUCATION'S HIERARCHY

Collaboration has been a recurring buzz word within schools for decades, primarily because it seems so consistent with education's periodic attempts to "empower" teachers and to engage them in "shared" or "participative" decision-making. The bad news is that our attempts ebb and flow from one decade to the next. The good news is that collaboration is happening in many schools. At the end of this chapter and those that follow, we describe representative programs and the processes the schools follow to organize and implement those programs.

Such collaborative programs are visible reassurance that "empowerment" is more than a buzz word; it is an essential component within the decisional activity of several schools across the country. Such schools have implemented these programs within a conceptual framework that goes well-beyond intuition, good intentions or guesswork. They result from well-integrated and internally-consistent theories that assure meaningful involvement of teachers and improved decision-making in schools.

"Collaboration" is sometimes extended to teachers as an administrative olive branch, an expression of mutual respect, a well-intentioned adjustment in school decision-making designed to promote human relations within the building. Sometimes it works; often it doesn't. Like other collegial activities, it works when it is integrated within the total system. It fails when it is poorly planned and becomes an extension of

1

extension of the system, a program operating on the periphery of traditional practice.

Consider the concepts of J. Edwards Deming, the world's leader in Quality Management and one of this country's foremost advocates of systems thinking. Deming has asserted for decades that all organizations must be looked at as total systems, that the functions of the system's components must be viewed not in isolation but in relation to each other. He suggests that only then can we understand the operation of the system and its relative success or failure. We discuss more of Deming's concepts later in this book.

For now, it's important that we accept Deming's notion that we can't look at decision-making in schools as an isolated phenomenon that occurs only at the top levels of the hierarchy or in occasional collaboration with teachers. It is an essential process that occurs throughout the system and that engages, either proactively or reactively, everyone in the system. According to Deming, problems within the system rarely result from individuals, but rather from a dysfunction of the system itself.

He suggests that not only teachers, but also administrators, are influenced by the systems within which they work. Just as teachers are sometimes restricted by managerial control and formal organizational structure, many administrators are restricted by similar characteristics. We have taught administration and supervision at the university level for decades and have been blessed with students who want to promote teacher autonomy and collaboration when they become practicing administrators. Many, perhaps most, will discover organizational obstacles in their attempts.

All of them have studied McGregor's concepts of Theory X and Theory Y, as well as Maslow's Hierarchy of Needs. All espouse the Theory Y principles of mutual trust and shared responsibility. All agree with Maslow's desire to help teachers satisfy their social and ego needs and, ultimately, realize increased self-actualization. Many, however, will find themselves unable to practice what McGregor and Maslow have preached.

They will bump into system practices that remain rooted in the past, that pose problems for even the most forward-thinking administrator. Their attempts to help teachers move along the professional growth continuum from potential to self-actualization will be hampered by organizational factors that threaten the security and social needs of teachers. Their Theory Y behaviors will be compromised by Theory X processes and procedures within the system. Like Deming, many will find insight in a paraphrase of Shakespeare: "The fault lies in our systems, not in ourselves."

This first section, then, focuses on possible reasons for the occasional dysfunction of education's hierarchy. It looks at characteristics of the hierarchical system that manage to interfere with substantive change and satisfying relationships within schools. It then provides specific examples of programs in schools that have overcome these problems by promoting increased levels of collaboration between administrators and others in the building. As important, it explains how these problems have been overcome.

THE ORIGINS OF THE HIERARCHY

The origins of education's hierarchy are rooted somewhere in the human need to assert ascendancy over others. This need is as natural as the playground pecking order or the Park Avenue social register and as enduring as inner city gangs and suburban country clubs. Call it "turf," "status," or "position," the desire for ascendancy over others characterizes human beings of all ages and stations. The hierarchies that result are found in every social institution from the family to the school system and all share common characteristics.

They all involve a protocol of behaviors that emphasize ordered relationships and routine predictability. Well before renowned German sociologist Max Weber asserted the need for graded levels of authority in bureaucratic organizations, hierarchies were evident everywhere, rewarding the fortunate over the not-so-fortunate, the bright over the not-so-bright, the aggressive over the passive, and the strong over the weak.

Those occupying the highest levels of the hierarchy invariably sustain their positions and maintain the organization by requiring predictable behaviors from those below. In the case of bureaucratic organizations, such predictability emphasizes not only the survival needs of hierarchical superiors but the rational nature of the system. In schools, such predictability is evidenced in everything from contract agreements and orientation programs to teacher assignments and policy books.

Hierarchies also provide deference and decisional authority to persons at the highest levels. In fact, such persons enjoy a broad range of authorities, many of which directly affect the freedoms of their subordinates. To maintain needed predictability, hierarchies often restrict the freedoms of persons within the organization. These freedoms and the issues of power they involve are the focus of this chapter.

THE PARADOX OF HIERARCHIES

George Bernard Shaw once defined democracy as a system that provides governance which is no better than people deserve. That Shaw's observation is correct and that we deserve bureaucracy and hierarchical organization seems historically evident. Both have been as inseparable from democracy in this country as the chain of command from the military, and, paradoxically, both sometimes restrict the very freedoms they were intended to complement.

Let's admit it, the democratic principles we cherish are sometimes compromised by the processes we choose to organize and deliver them. As desirable as these principles are in concept, therefore, they sometimes fall short in application. It would seem, then, that our delivery systems would require at least periodic scrutiny, not because they are bad—many of them have served us well over the years—but because they simply might serve us better.

Education's hierarchy, however, is rarely scrutinized. It is entrenched in our national psyche almost as firmly as democracy—and as routinely unchallenged. School organization provides a classic example. The rapid growth of educational administration at the turn of the century required a new model of organization for schools. The most obvious models at the time were the government, the military, and such emerging specifics as Max Weber's concepts of bureaucracy and Frederick Taylor's Principles of Scientific Management.

The hierarchy that resulted created variable levels of authority to coordinate the growing numbers of teachers and activities within schools. It also resulted in variable levels of status and decisional input, the highest levels enjoying the most status and exercising the most decisional input regarding the character of education's programs and culture. This practice has promoted several myths that continue to influence the organization and character of schools.

Myth Number One: "The upper levels of the hierarchy are occupied by the most experienced and most knowledgeable people in the school."

Early concepts of school administration created ordered relationships that capitalized on the superior technical competence of the "principal" teacher. He or she, usually he, was often the best teacher in the building and the logical person to guide the younger teachers and provide direction for the behavior of students, the development of curriculum, and the improvement of instruction.

Contemporary education, however, finds technical competence in all areas of the building. Fortunately, many of the superior teachers are still in the classroom, and most of the support personnel like counselors, social workers, and special educators, perform specialized responsibilities that few administrators can be expected to master. The inclination of the hierarchy in some schools, therefore, to attribute superior technical competence of only administrators disregards the changing nature of professional responsibilities and the routine involvement of others in the building who have the special expertise to refine curriculum, improve teaching, and identify and meet the changing needs of students.

The arena of decision-making, therefore, seems to remain predominantly, sometimes exclusively, in the offices and meeting rooms of administrators. Teachers often enter this arena on an input rather than a decisional basis. As such, they remain spectators, less often participants, in decisional processes. It seems that tradition has sanctioned organizational practices that no longer reflect the needs of the organizations. That this has happened is not too surprising.

TAKING ANOTHER LOOK AT OUR ORIGINS

Let's revisit just one of Frederick Taylor's Principles of Scientific Management. A forerunner in the field of management, recognized and renowned for his early contributions, Frederick Taylor asserted in his book, *Shop Management* (published by Harper's in 1911), "Managers should plan; workers should work." It was a principle that abstracted the essence of Taylor's philosophy, the belief that effective management was the result of time studies and control of workers by management.

This principle, and the others in his book also reflected the prevailing social relationships of the times. The United States at the turn of the century was experiencing a level of social elitism that may not have been new to us but that was being reinforced by a variety of writers, only one of whom was Frederick Taylor. Consider the philosophy of the Dean of American Sportswriters, Caspar Whitney, when he wrote in *A Sporting Pilgrimage* (Harper's, 1894):

> Why there should be such constant strife to bring together in sport the two divergent elements in society that never by chance meet elsewhere on even terms is quite incomprehensible, and it is altogether the sole cause of all our athletic woe. . . . The laboring class are all right in their way; let them go their way in peace, and have their athletics in whatsoever manner best suits their inclinations. . . . Let us have our sport among the more refined elements.

Early educational administration was influenced by such thinking. This is not to say that teachers were perceived necessarily as "lower-class" citizens, but they were, and maybe are, considered the working class in the building. Certainly, the several teacher strikes that occur every fall in America suggest adversarial divisions of management and labor in many of our schools. And equally certain, many schools continue to practice Frederick Taylor's premise that managers should plan and workers should work.

We are not implying that today's schools are subject to the rigid social proscriptions of the turn of the century. We are suggesting, however, that a method of organization born at that time promotes relationships that fail to acknowledge broad-based technical competence in schools. Persons new to administration are necessarily influenced by a method of organization that, according to Max Weber, involves a well-defined hierarchy of authority that assumes responsibility for decision-making.

Such persons are induced to assume roles that ostensibly determine the direction of the organization, to feel the burden of making tough decisions, and to expect the status that comes with such responsibility. They generally are disinclined to create processes that promote broad-based decision-making and to recognize the technical competence of superior teachers who are best qualified to make decisions about curriculum and their own professional growth.

THE INTRANSIGENCE OF TRADITION

That education seems so unable to break this grip of tradition is not surprising. Even a basic understanding of systems theory suggests that all systems try to maintain equilibrium, that is, they seek "steady states." Our bodies seek a constant temperature, and our cars require a steady mixture of gas and air. When either of these changes, even insignificantly, the system experiences disequilibrium—and risks potential trouble.

Though usually bad for our bodies and our cars, disequilibrium is sometimes good for school systems, particularly when they require alternate ways of making decisions. The point is, they won't make these changes themselves; by definition, systems are resistant to change. According to systems theorists, they all have regulatory processes that help maintain the steady states that are so resistant to change.

Interestingly, one of the feedback processes in schools involves the teachers themselves. Tradition has sanctioned administrative decision-making for so long that teachers have grown to expect it, even to the point of questioning the courage and charisma of principals who open up the process to the rest of the school. Some teachers even expect to give deference to hierarchical superiors and are uncomfortable in peer-oriented relationships. This was true in the beginning of the change process at Bass School which is profiled at the end of this chapter.

THE NEED FOR RATIONALITY

Much of this relates to expectations of rationality within the system, a focus of many early theorists of educational administration. They reasoned that organizations are more efficient when emotions are not a factor in planning and decision-making. Reflecting early Victorianism, these theorists, and the organizations that resulted from their thinking, failed to acknowledge the fundamental psychological and social needs that people bring to work each day. A result was the sometimes apparent failure of organizations to achieve all their goals.

Myth Number Two: "Most schools operate and should be expected to operate in purely rational ways."

Famed industrialist J.P. Morgan once said that people have two reasons for doing anything—a good reason and the real reason. You and we can be quite certain that education's real reason for its occasional failure to achieve its goals has something to do with emotion. This anonymous quote provides further insight: "[When emotions are] encouraged, they perfume life; discouraged, they poison it." Relationships within organizations, therefore, can invariably be poisoned when rationality is expected to prevail, especially to the exclusion of the feelings that are inevitable when people interact and seek their satisfactions in work.

Tradition is hard to beat. Expectations of rationality and hierarchical relationships keep teachers on a continuum that simply highlights the degree of their dependency. According to prominent theorists, teachers are found on a continuum that ranges not from hierarchical to collaborative, but from most hierarchical to least hierarchical (Sergiovanni & Starrett, 1988). One might reason that the "least hierarchical" end of the continuum involves the most collaboration. Such reasoning, however, can be misleading.

Many administrators attempt to reduce the effects of the hierarchy by relating benignly to teachers or assuming a laissez faire approach to decision-making. They do little to promote teacher autonomy—or to lessen the impact of the school's hierarchy. A decrease in teacher dependency doesn't necessarily increase teacher autonomy. Research has indicated for years that some dependent teachers can become autonomous (Carpenter, 1971).

Others, perhaps most, replace or complement dependency with isolation, alienation, or indifference (Argyris, 1955). The reduction of hierarchical organization, therefore, does not necessarily promote collaboration and teacher autonomy. To the contrary, some teachers liberated from the protocols of the hierarchy become confused. When introduced to collaboration for the first time, they sometimes see its "opportunity" as an uncharted course. The destination is described by others as desirable, but only a few people know how to reach it.

Administrators, therefore, who seek to lessen the impact of the hierarchy by "making friends" with teachers, or by assuming a "hands-off" approach to activities within the building, do little to promote collaboration—or to lessen the impact of the hierarchy. They fail to realize that alternative structures are needed to engage teachers in collaborative processes that provide the conditions for their growth toward autonomy and that result in qualitatively better decisions within the building.

COLLABORATION IN ITS BROADEST SENSE

Think of it this way. Anyone who seeks dependent or autonomous behaviors in others is well-advised to study Figure 1.1. If each range of characteristics does exist on a continuum, the question is, where do schools interested in collaboration find themselves? A second, equally important question involves the expectations of administrators. Where are they on a continuum from autocratic to collaborative?

The obvious answer is that school administrators can be found anywhere on the continuum. By philosophical predisposition, many of them—maybe most—are on the collaborative end; at least they want to be. The traditional isolation of teachers from decisions involving the heart and soul of their classrooms is not primarily the fault of administrators. We have already indicated that hierarchies resulted from the unprecedented growth of schools at the turn of the century. The chain of command, therefore, was forged by the intensity of its own growth. Today, this "steady state" is acknowledged in many schools as much for its inflexibility as its strength (Abbott & Lovell, 1965).

FIGURE 1.1. AUTONOMY VS. DEPENDENCY

Autonomy	Dependency
Withhold information	Share information
Restrict decision-making	Share decision-making
Establish narrow range of acceptable behaviors	Establish optimal expectations of behavior
Condition thinking	Encourage thinking
Reward conformity and punish nonconformity	Accommodate diversity
Obscure individual differences	Promote individual differences
Depersonalize environment	Personalize environment
Sustain threat	Eliminate threat
Affirm layers of control	Reduce layers of control
Marginally affiliate with colleagues	Closely affiliate with colleagues
Closely affiliate with authority	Marginally affiliate with authority
Maintain external locus of control	Encourage internal locus of control

THE RISE OF COLLEGIALITY

That tradition carries a double-edged sword to enforce education's steady-state is a disturbing, but evident, reality to those of us seeking change in decisional processes. Yet, such changes are occurring, slowly but steadily, in some instances, dramatically. That they are occurring slowly may be frustrating to eager young teachers waiting expectantly on the edge of substantive decision-making, but it is heartening to those of us who realize that sudden change in education rarely survives.

Collegiality, the process of peers helping peers, though a reality in schools for many years, is still evolving, slowly influencing the philosophies and behaviors of teachers and administrators alike. In schools where "Collegial Consultation," "Cognitive Coaching," "Peer Mentoring," or "Collegial Supervision" have survived, teachers have been introduced gradually to the concepts and behaviors that assure their success. When introduced overnight, such programs, normally trends, rarely gain a foothold and die almost as dramatically as they were conceived.

Trends in some schools are the organizational equivalent of fast food. They appear and disappear in a flurry of activity, leave everyone undernourished, and are immediately forgotten in the next frenzied search for new ideas. Unfortunately, administrators in many schools are interested in trends more for their public relations value than their potential to improve the school's program. We discuss this notion at more length in a later chapter. For now, it's important to realize the failure of many schools to influence the philosophies and skills of teachers and administrators and to discuss their needs before implementing new programs.

Consider, for example, the popular practice of introducing administrators to the basics of new concepts such as collaborative supervision, then introducing the programs to the teaching staff just before implementing them. Such programs are condemned to failure by an inherent contradiction in the process. The administration's attempt to lessen the impact of the hierarchy by introducing a collaborative program only affirms the hierarchy's power by failing to plan and implement the program collaboratively!

Such administrative predispositions to act unilaterally are only one reason why teachers are unaccustomed to collaboration in schools. Not only do administrators introduce such programs without prior consultation with teachers, but they are unable to promote activities that influence the willingness and skills of teachers to behave in "collaborative ways." Effective collaboration involves a sophisticated set of skills that enable people to share ideas in accepting and nonthreatening ways, to be encouraging and cooperatively analytic, in essence to create the kind of synergy that results in increased organizational effectiveness.

Such skills must be developed. Discussing them with teachers in in-service training activities is only one of the first steps schools must take to introduce new programs. Appropriate supervision activities must then be developed to assure that teachers have the follow-up opportunities to "practice what someone else has preached." This step often takes one or more years. Only when teachers have accepted the philosophies that underlie such programs and have developed the behaviors that bring such philosophies to life can new programs have a fighting chance in schools.

Additionally, our society can't expect teachers to collaborate in program planning and professional growth activities when many school hierarchies practice noncollaborative, even unilateral, decision-making. All programs new to schools involve new behaviors, some more sophisticated than others. This constitutes one of the primary reasons why such programs must be given time to develop. In essence, to be successful, trends require new behaviors, and new behaviors require time to develop.

Also, time is required to assess organizational needs, to involve teachers in early planning stages, and to assure the collaborative development of goals, objectives, and solution elements. Planners must anticipate obstacles and find or create ways to overcome them. They must develop materials to bring programs to life and monitoring procedures to assure that programs are doing what they were designed to do. And, most importantly, they must provide inservice training activities that promote the development of the behaviors teachers will need to assure the program's success.

SOME REPRESENTATIVE PROGRAMS

Teachers and administrators in many schools across the country have become so collaborative that they are not only sharing information and decision-making but eliminating the threat that sometimes accompanies hierarchical relationships. In essence, the teachers in the schools that emphasize collaborative activities find themselves relating to administrators as peers. As suggested in Figure 1.1, they are marginally affiliated with the school's authority structure and closely affiliated with colleagues, even when such colleagues occupy administrative roles.

Autonomy thrives in the same climate that nourishes collaboration, in an atmosphere of interaction and mutual trust. Fortunately, such concepts are alive and well in contemporary education. The representative programs, profiled in succeeding chapters, engage teachers in the general decisional activity of the building. They are outstanding in the sense that they have broken down traditional barriers to open communication and to teacher involvement in the school's general operation. Bass Elementary School in Chicago is one such example.

BASS ELEMENTARY SCHOOL
CHICAGO, ILLINOIS

COLLABORATIVE COMPONENTS

- Engages students and parents in decision-making
- Partners with an MBA program of a major university to learn and implement a quality improvement process
- Incorporates parents in problem-solving
- School Improvement Plan and accompanying budget are developed by teachers
- Practices site-based management through the Local School Council (LSC)

OVERVIEW

Bass Elementary School shines and brings hope to the torn, neglected Englewood neighborhood of Chicago's inner city. It's walls burst with 829 students in prekindergarten through eighth grade. Parents plead to be on the waiting list of this neighborhood school where the only entrance constraint is enough space. In spite of its neighborhood popularity, the student turnover rate is 78%. Yet, despite the odds and a history of test scores that fall well below the national norm, Bass Elementary School can now boast success. The story of Bass' turnaround in student achievement is worth telling.

Marcie Gillie had taught in the Chicago system for many years before she was persuaded to come to Bass Elementary School in 1983. She was reluctant to take on the role of principal, she says, because her leadership style was definitely not the typical bureaucratic "tell them what to do." As she tells it, there were frustrating times in the years ahead as she worked to develop the trust that would encourage

discussions and even healthy disagreements over instructional strategies and a host of other issues impacting student
success.

In the Fall of 1991, Gillie was one of six Chicago principals selected to engage in a series of conversations with a
group of Chicago's top corporate executives on how they
might support school improvement. About the fourth or fifth
meeting they were joined by the director of one of the
nation's renown business schools, Northwestern University's
Kellogg School of Management. Kellogg's vision of "Creating
World-Class Quality" was explained, and the possibility of
Total Quality Improvement's applicability to public education was pondered. At the conclusion of the next meeting,
the six principals were invited to a week of executive leadership training at Northwestern's Allen Center where they
joined 50 leaders from all over the world.

No changes were made to the training format and the
educators were asked to experience and debrief with suggestions for adaptation to their settings.

In the Fall of 1992, with extensive groundwork having
been done to engage staff and parents, 23 Chicago Schools
committed to the quality learning project, with another 14
schools to be added the following year. In addition to
intensive summer training, participating schools received on-
site assistance of two graduate students and a faculty
member in the Kellogg program. There was also a schedule
of weekend day-retreats throughout the year for the school
teams.

As this unique partnership has developed and flourished
over the past several years, significant changes have occurred
at Bass Elementary School, enabling student achievement to
rise, and for teachers, parents and students to work as a team
to make the learning decisions collaboratively.

PROGRAM HIGHLIGHTS

Bass Elementary School adapted the Plan-Do-Study-Act
process developed by Deming and adapted by other leaders
in the quality field. Under the tutelage of Northwestern's

graduate management students, they were asked to select and gather decision data for two problems, one that would be relatively easy to address (low hanging fruit is the vernacular of the quality movement) and one that would be much harder to define and effect improvement. Bass chose to improve school security because of the increasing neighborhood dangers. For the tough issue, they chose to improve seventh and eighth graders respect for each other and the adults in their lives. These were the beginning "practice problems" selected by the initial quality team in order to "hit the ground running." In following years, teachers and students would prioritize their list of improvements to be addressed by various teams. At the end of year two, Bass counted 220 improvement activities that were carried out as implementations of the objectives in their school design.

Chicago schools, as part of reform legislation enacted 6 years ago, use site-based management which means Local School Councils, which are composed of six parents, two teachers, two community members, and the principal, are empowered to plan and operate their schools around their own vision. School Improvement Plans and a State of Illinois Quality Review Process are linked to school and student outcomes. Individual schools, however, may choose their own process of operating within the broad guidelines. Using the quality improvement process, and concentrating on problem-solving that focuses on system improvements, Bass Elementary School posted a 70% reduction in seventh grade failures the first year as they responded to their "tough issue." An additional 300% increase in the number of students who made the "A Honors List" was noted. In reflecting, they could see the changing culture for students. "It's okay to strive for A's. It's okay to take home books!" "We go to a quality school," was the word out in the neighborhood.

THE PROCESS

Bass created six design teams, all of which include a mix of teachers, parents, and students. The teams are broad-based umbrellas for improving climate, parent involvement, student achievement, attendance, and academic processes. The teams meet as a whole once a month to share and ask support (often very specific) from other teams. When the School Improvement Plan is reviewed and redesigned with the budget process, they all work together as well. Otherwise, teams meet at varying times. It is part of the Bass culture that all students have 90 minutes a week for pleasure reading and as one of many creative solutions to meeting times, parent volunteers free teachers to meet. Curriculum teams make their own decisions and always work to ensure that there is cross-team collaboration. This school, typical of many in the quality movement, uses themes to integrate the disciplines and project learning as a major strategy for engaging students as active learners. For example, the language arts and science teams combine each year for the annual Bass kite flying exhibit. Students design their own kites, according to scientific principles, and in the course of the project they demonstrate it, write about it, and share with families and the community.

Another example of the quality process in action occurred when Bass got a new student lunchroom and had to figure out a way to eat for one whole term in the auditorium. When the plan (developed by faculty, students, and parents) was finally tried the first time, each person entering the auditorium on that day got a 3x5 card on which they were asked, "What is wrong with our process? What is not working for you?" The design team collected the cards, went back to the planning table, and worked out the "problems" in the new lunchroom process. For the rest of the term, the lunch program ran smoothly. To report on the first "low hanging fruit" improvement, that of improving school security, visitors to Bass will now be greeted by parents who serve as hall monitors. A Parent Patrol, replete with walkie-talkies for communication, helps ensure safe passage to and from school in the neighborhood.

Central to any school-adapted process of quality improvement is, of course, improving instruction. Northwestern's training currently uses William Glasser's , *The Quality School: Managing Students Without Coercion,* as the framework from which Bass Elementary School faculty assess their learning climate and instructional program. Bass faculty learned, and now apply, Glasser's Control Theory Principles—the basic needs of all living things:

survival (give students hope for better things)

love (tell them each day that you love them)

power (provide some control over what happens to them)

fun (make learning interesting and fun)

freedom (provide opportunities for choices)

belonging (use team-building and cooperative learning strategies)

Another book recommended by Bass faculty as instrumental in improving their teaching is the ASCD book *Multiple Intelligences in the Classroom* by Thomas Armstrong.

The importance of the quality process, according to Gillie and the Bass Local School Council, is that there is no beginning and no end. Quality is circular as implemented. It is a continuous improvement process that encourages risk-taking, where criticism is freely given because it is always directed to the system, not the valued people in the system.

WHAT CAN WE LEARN?

Marcie Gillie, Bass Elementary School's former principal, is now engaged in bringing successful quality implementation to Chicago schools who make the commitment. She has a small office on Northwestern's campus, but you will find her there only rarely. She is most often in the schools or conducting teacher training for improving instruction in the classroom.

Her phone line is always open to the Kellogg graduate students or the range of people in the schools who are working to improve learning. She reflects on one of the major learnings for principals and teachers who want to flatten the hierarchy. They need to know, understand, and apply lead-management as opposed to boss-management. Glasser is very specific about the differences. Lead-management uses persuasion and problem-solving as central to leadership. The lead manager (principal and teacher) spends time and energy to determine how to run the system so workers want to do quality work. Boss-management, on the other hand, limits quality of work, limits productivity of the worker, and actually produces most of the discipline problems we are trying to prevent. It is Gillies' contention that true collaboration, whether in schools using quality or other processes, will not succeed unless the seeds have been sown for lead-management and the participants understand the difference between the two.

Bass Elementary School also serves as an example of the group most often left out of shared decision-making, the students. Gillie likes to tell the story of one of her student briefings when she would report to the students about the Northwestern training, about the quality issues being discussed in the LSC (Local School Council), and other school issues. The common practice was to start with the eighth grade, and bring in the next grade every half hour until all grades had been briefed. She asked the older grades if they knew what a "quality dismissal" would be and could they effect one as they left the auditorium. Could they actually do it all by themselves, without directions from any adult? "Yes," they answered, and this proceeded through each grade until the third grade was leaving and a single student turned and waived to her second grade friend. A second-grader piped up, "Mrs. Gillie, that was not a quality dismissal because one person didn't do her part." The second grade then proceeded with a "perfect, quality dismissal."

SCHOOL STATISTICS

Perkins Bass Elementary School
Chicago, Illinois

Principal: Kathryn Kemp

Number of Students: 829
Grades: Prekindergarten through eighth grade

Number of faculty: 100 (including support and volunteer staff)

REFERENCES

Abbott, M.G., and J.T. Lovell, eds. 1965. *Change perspectives in educational administration*. Auburn, AL: School of Education, Auburn University.

Argyris, C. 1964. *Integrating the individual and the organization*. New York: John Wiley and Sons.

Carpenter, H.H. "Formal Organizational structural factors and perceived job satisfaction of classroom teachers." *Administrative Science Quarterly*.

Sergiovanni, T. and R. Starrett. 1993. *Supervision: A redefinition*. New York: McGraw-Hill.

Taylor, F.W. 1911. *Shop management*. New York: Harper.

Whitney, C. 1894. *A sporting pilgrimage*. New York: Harper.

Parts of this chapter were reprinted with permission of the Helen Dwight Reid Educational Foundation from Koehler, M. "Teacher autonomy: just how far have we come?" *The Clearing House*, Vol. 64, Sept./Oct. 1990, pp. 51–53, published by Heldref Publications, 1319 18th St., NW, Washington, DC 20036–1802.

2

THE HIERARCHY'S INVISIBLE ORGANIZATION

When Trogar crawled from his cave one morning with the unprecedented notion of becoming the head of his clan, he wasn't really sure how to go about it. In fact, he was uncertain about what he wanted to do. All he knew was that it was time the clan got organized and that he was the guy to do it. He realized that he wasn't the clan's best hunter; heck, he didn't even like hunting. He couldn't see himself hunting for the rest of his life anyway. But he felt confident that he would enjoy being the principal clansperson; something about the idea intrigued him.

Thus began the *visible* organizational hierarchy—etched in stone as it were. And like so many of his administrative successors, Trogar's desire to lead the clan probably was only marginally altruistic. Part of him must have realized the advantages of coordinating the clan to improve the gathering and distribution of food, the maintenance of the caves, and protection from saber-toothed tigers.

Another part of him, however, enjoyed the thought of putting his desk in the biggest cave and having clanspersons call him *Mr.* Trogar. The clan may have believed that hunting was its most important activity, but "leading" seemed to be growing in popularity, despite everyone's confusion about the term. Trogar was convinced that the time had come to resolve the confusion by helping the clan "get organized."

He soon discovered that his status lasted only as long as his new position. Because Trogar was history's first principal clansperson, getting the job was relatively easy. Keeping it, however, became increasingly difficult as other clanspersons realized the advantages of status. A respect that had accrued formerly only to hunters, those experts in the clan who assumed the daily task of assuring survival of the clan's culture, was now being shared—in dinosaur doses—with Trogar and his growing cadre of assistant principal clanspersons.

As a result, Trogar and his assistants soon found themselves more interested in surviving as the leaders of the clan than in managing its resources and protection. Thus was born the *invisible* organizational hierarchy. Trogar did such a good job creating it that, like the visible organization, it has persisted to the present day.

EDUCATION'S INVISIBLE ORGANIZATION

We can find an invisible organization operating in every school system. It involves fundamentally the same relationships as in the visible, formal organization, but its decisions are less concerned with the normative values of the school than with the survival needs of the persons within it. Certainly, survival is a key word in any organization. As the organization goes, so go the people within it. It follows, therefore, that any decisions within the organization are made—to some extent—to enhance the status of the decision-makers. This was one of Trogar's first learning experiences.

Had he been the principal clansperson of a school system, he also would have learned that schools invariably bite off more than they can chew. It's not that schools have an enormous appetite for change. To the contrary, schools can be among society's most intransigent institutions. More likely, most of them suffer from someone's expectations to sample the menu that normally is placed before them.

Generally, that "someone" is the school's administration in conjunction with the board of education. Interestingly, the activities that result from such "menu-planning," though created by the school's *visible* organization, more nearly reflect the needs of the *invisible* organization. See Figure 2.1 for a description of their contrasting characteristics.

FIGURE 2.1. EDUCATION'S VISIBLE AND INVISIBLE ORGANIZATIONS

Visible	Invisible
Concerned with reality	Concerned with appearance
Seeks solutions to problems	Responds to "trends"
Appears selfless	Is selfish
Provides professional status	Guarantees personal status
Appears proactive	Is reactive
Form controls function	Function controls form
Relies on expert power	Relies on hierarchical power
Advances school's goals	Advances personal position
Seeks institutional survival	Seeks personal survival
Administration help organization	Organization helps administration
Advances public responsibility	Advances public relations

The menu itself consists of a range of desirable and healthy items, usually the current trends that are found in so much of the literature. Recently, such items have included higher order thought process, questioning techniques, cooperative learning, reflective teaching, authentic assessment, block scheduling, and a range of teaching strategies. They are important items, because they are so consistent with the normative values of the visible organization of every school system.

It is the *invisible* organization, however, which orders and serves them. Therein lies the problem—and the focus of this chapter. Consider the example of a local high school. Each year, it develops several goals to guide the planning and professional growth activities of the staff. The goals are then broken down into objectives for each department within the school with related in-service activities scheduled for the staff throughout the year.

So far so good. The school even brings in consultants to work with the staff as they develop follow-up activities for each objective. It would seem that the school's hierarchy is doing all it can to accommodate one or more of the concepts that have been identified in the literature as so important for our nation's schools. That the process is more responsive, however, to the survival needs of the hierarchy than to the normative values of the school is evident in the reactions of one of the teachers.

"Last year, it was authentic assessment; this year, it's block scheduling. We didn't even scratch the surface of authentic assessment last year, and we probably won't make a dent in block scheduling this year. Before we get a handle on one idea, we're working on another. Why are we doing this anyway?"

Good question. It's a question asked each year by thousands of teachers across the country. The answer involves a close look at the visible and the invisible organizations in schools. Let's review why planning and professional growth goals are developed by schools each year. The visible organization develops them because they hold the potential for improved teaching and are in the best interests of students. At least that's what most administrators claim.

The invisible organization develops such goals, however, because they seem educationally desirable and involve "high-profile" activities within the school community. They are "proof positive" to parents, board members, and district superiors that the school's administration is on the "cutting edge" of current research and is deserving of recognition, financial support, and an elevated position in the school's culture.

Most school administrators realize that the sharing of annual goals with the parent community tells parents what they want to hear and ultimately reinforces the status of the school's decision-makers. They also acknowledge that such goals have merit in their own right because they seek to improve the school's curriculum, instructional program, and ancillary services. They have learned that educationally desirable goals are especially effective when such goals also enhance the personal and professional status of persons in the hierarchy.

Successful administrators realize the public relations value of visionary planning activities in the school. They acknowledge the need to continually improve the programs and the competencies of school professionals, and they recognize the personal benefit of being identified by parents and organizational superiors as leaders who help the school toward the realization of such worthy goals.

Obviously, nothing is wrong with providing effective—and broadly recognized—leadership. After all, every successful public relations effort consists of four essential steps: one, do something noteworthy; two, tell everybody; three, tell everybody; and four, tell everybody. Problems arise when school administrators "tell everybody" but fail to do something noteworthy. That the invisible organization sometimes embraces goals more for the opportunity to "tell everybody" than to contribute to the normative values of the school is usually evident in the activities designed to accomplish them.

WHAT ARE THE PURPOSES OF IN-SERVICE TRAINING PROGRAMS?

Most school in-service training programs are mandated by state agencies. Sometimes they are designed to assist teachers and others in the building in realizing the school's annual goals. Often, they are not. Usually, they result from committees that have been asked to develop an in-service program for the year, and, most often, they are ineffective.

The actual activities are usually restricted to the number required by the state and are entertaining, but inadequate, ways to influence teacher behavior. They tend to be one-shot presentations that are rarely integrated with the other aspects of the school's professional growth program. Rarely do teachers get follow-up opportunities to "practice what someone else has preached."

A result is that the fruits of valuable research rarely fail to find their way into the nation's classrooms with any degree of consistency. It's not surprising, then, that so many of today's hot new ideas are yesterday's trends—similar ideas with different names. Twenty years ago, we studied shared decision-making, decentralization, and variable modular scheduling. Today, we're looking at teacher empowerment, site-based management, and block scheduling. Not much has changed—identical ideas, different names.

The repetition of this "trend cycle" means simply that the ideas are good. They must be; they keep recurring. What is bad is how schools seek to implement them. The invisible organization is one of the culprits. As long as it encourages school administrators to embrace valuable new concepts in education more for their public relations value than for their ability to improve the quality of classroom instruction, most American schools will remain rooted in traditional methodologies regardless of the ability of such methodologies to promote learning.

This disinclination to provide adequate follow-up activities to the presentation of new ideas is a further illustration of the motives of the invisible organization. Let's admit it; rarely do schools provide comprehensive professional growth activities which enable teachers to *functionally* integrate the ideas of visiting experts. It would seem, then, that many in-service programs serve only to satisfy state-mandated expectations and to impress the local parent community.

Less often do they make a significant and lasting impression on the instructional behaviors of teachers or on the operation of the school. Were they intended to help teachers grow professionally, teachers would not be "lectured at" once every 2 or 3 months; they would be given opportunities to learn the concepts and integrate them into their instructional repertoires. Such learning experiences for teachers would be more consistent with the normative values of the school system because they would positively influence the learning of students.

WHO ARE THE CLIENTS OF OUR SCHOOLS?

An important aspect of the issue, therefore, involves this critical question: Who are the clients of our schools? The visible organization regards students as the primary clients; the invisible organization focuses on parents and other authority figures in the community and the district hierarchy. If restructuring, another recent catchword (remember "organizational design" 20 years ago?), is to experience any success, educators will have to acknowledge the existence of the invisible organization and be willing to do something about it.

Restructuring is a recurring topic that receives attention from significant persons in education, including the Department of Education. Of all the trends that receive a fleeting moment of front-cover stardom on educational journals, it seems to hold the greatest promise for significant change in education. But it, too, is likely to flop just after opening night if its promoters fail to consider the behind-the-scenes influences on its performance, particularly from such powerful influences as education's invisible organization.

CHANGE IS NOT AN ILLUSION

The invisible organization has been influential ever since Trogar invented ways to secure his position as principal clansperson. It is just as powerful today in many of the nation's schools, for many of the same reasons. Fortunately, many schools across the country have dispelled George Bernard Shaw's contention that "change is an illusion." They have reduced the influence of the invisible organization by reasserting the fundamental purposes of the visible organization and by engaging teachers in the planning that transforms desirable trends into educational realities.

Who would have guessed, certainly not Trogar, that millions of years later, hordes of systems theorists would explain his search for clan supremacy in terms of "progressive segregation." Systems thinkers defined it as the separation of an undifferentiated whole into differentiated causal chains, each having specific functions to perform. What results is a hierarchy of responsibilities. From ant colonies to suburban high schools, such responsibilities involve both leaders and workers in the performance of clearly defined tasks.

Myth Number Three: "Many school systems in this country range from most bureaucratic/hierarchical to most collaborative."

Much of the literature would have us believe that recent trends toward collegial supervision and site-based management have transformed school organizations from purely hierarchical to collaborative and peer-oriented. We are led to believe that many schools have abandoned centralized decision-making and are engaging the majority of staff in collaborative, teacher-empowered activities that necessarily increase organizational synergy.

Tom Sergiovanni, one of education's most prominent writers, however, asserts in his book, *Supervision, A Redefinition* (1993), that schools range not from most hierarchical to most collaborative but from most hierarchical to *least* hierarchical. Progressive segregation, therefore, continues to influence the nature of the relationships in schools and to determine the impact of the organization on the behaviors and the sense of autonomy of teachers.

The challenge to all of us is to find ways to break from this deterministic impact of systems theory. Fortunately, some schools are doing just that. They have devised processes that allow "progressively segregated" schools to function effectively in communities that also value the synergy resulting from "progressively integrating" mutually cooperative if occasionally conflicting ideas. They recognize that the differentiation of roles does not imply a differentiation of intelligent ideas.

As noted in Figure 2.1, such schools emphasize the characteristics of the visible organization. School personnel plan proactively and aggressively seek solutions to problems. The school focuses on its goals (form) and uses them to determine the processes (function) they will use to realize the goals. They actually avoid ritualized processes (functions) that subordinate the goals (form) of the school. Most importantly, the administration helps the school by relying on the expert power found not only in the principal's office but throughout the building.

Such administrators avoid a preoccupation with "trends," are concerned more with reality than appearance, forego exclusive reliance on hierarchical authority, and are unconcerned about using the organization to advance their personal position and sense of status. Their behavior reflects a genuine desire to realize the normative values of the school and to satisfy the human needs of both students and teachers. The College School profiled in this chapter is an outstanding example.

Myth Number Four: "Persons occupying positions in the hierarchy are not only organizationally superior to others in the building but are better than they in many ways."

Henry Murray told us decades ago that all of us have ego needs that must be satisfied if we are to achieve a sense of self. He indicated that we all seek *achievement*, the need to accomplish something difficult, *counteraction*, the need to overcome a weakness in oneself, *understanding*, the need to master a body of knowledge, and *sensuous experience*, the need to be involved in events.

To the extent that schools fail to provide opportunities for the satisfaction of such needs in teachers, they disregard their growth needs and compromise their effectiveness in the class- room. They also fail to benefit from the collective expertise of scores of teachers who understand the nuances of the teaching- learning process and feel a strong sense of commitment to satisfy these same needs in students. In essence, teachers who are unable to satisfy their own ego needs may be equally unable to satisfy the ego needs of their students.

The invisible organization is generally unconcerned about the ego needs of teachers and students. Such an organization values teachers who create high-profile programs more for their public relations value than for their potential to promote the goals of the school. Administrators of such schools are more concerned with their person positions and generally engage in the kinds of "status charades" that Max Abbott described several decades ago in his article "Hierarchical Impediments to Innovation in Educational Organizations."

We all know such administrators. They actively seek status and behave in ways that pronounce not only their hierarchical but their personal superiority. They don't do much for the needs of students and teachers. The essential characteristic of successful school administrators, therefore, is to empower the visible organization, in essence to sustain a focus on the normative values of the school, which includes a relative disregard for themselves and a service to the others in the school with and for whom they work. Now meet Jan Phillips, our "definition" of a successful administrator.

THE COLLEGE SCHOOL
WEBSTER GROVES, MISSOURI

COLLABORATIVE COMPONENTS

The College School of Webster Groves, Missouri, practices empowerment with all of the stakeholders, including teachers, students and parents.

- Teachers develop their curriculum collaboratively for a thematic/experiential approach with an interdisciplinary, adventure-based focus
- Teams of teachers share equally in the hiring process for new staff
- A Faculty Issues Committee plans with the director playing an equal, collaborative role; responsibility for results rests with the team
- Teachers control most of the discretionary budget (not allocated to salaries and maintenance). They choose among additional curricular supports, field trips, anything they feel is essential to or enhancing the learning process
- This empowered faculty was selected as a Danforth network participant, a group of public, private, urban and suburban schools committed to understanding and leading the change process

OVERVIEW

Sometimes the challenge for leaders is not to bring about change to flatten the hierarchy, but to sustain the vision, the dream of an educational environment that has been developed and shared over time with parents, faculty, and students. Such is the story of The College School of Webster Groves, Missouri. The College School, having celebrated its 30th anniversary in 1992–93, is small (giving credibility to the research that smaller is better?), only 218 students, prekindergarten through eighth grade. Its curriculum is adventure-based, thematic, and highly experiential. Director Jan Phillips, who began her 6th year as director in 1994–95, began as a teacher at The College School 29 years ago.

In describing the curriculum, Phillips emphasizes the "we" in developing: faculty not only make the decisions, but they develop the content and theme-based experiences that begin in Kindergarten with a day in the woods. It is policy that the College's board of directors handle the financial oversight; they are not involved in curricular decisions. The school's philosophy is reflected by teachers who are empowered to develop the learning experiences. They work together in cross-grade-level teams. Currently, there are no texts; there is support for "not just one way, but many," and the themes selected are heavy in science and social studies, with carefully planned integration of math, communication, fine arts and other content areas.

As an adventure-based school, beginning in Kindergarten, there is a continuing exploration of the world, symbolized by the world map logo used in written communications. "Confidence, Creativity, and Competence" is The College School motto. Their mission is realized in seeking out and encouraging individual strengths while educating the whole child.

For 30 years, The College School has been noted for its outstanding experiential curriculum. Even before the Danforth connection, public and private schools throughout the world visited and learned from this model. The preschool program is unique to the St. Louis area. The curriculum is modeled in part after the preschools of Reggio Emilia, Italy, world renown for excellence in early childhood education. Many faculty have visited this Italian town to learn firsthand of Reggio's innovative techniques. The approach encourages the child's natural curiosity by provoking his or her ability to wonder, explore and hypothesize within a nurturing environment.

PROGRAM HIGHLIGHTS

Thematic, adventure-based highlights in grade level sequence include:

Kindergarten—Exploration begins with a day in the woods and reflecting on the experience using inventive spelling and/or dictating the experience.

First Grade—An overnight camp-out in the spring of the year in a local park focuses on observing and experiencing a new environment.

Second and Third Graders camp-out in the fall in a local state park, again integrating math and science in hands-on experiences and encompassing the other disciplines in follow-up reflections.

Fourth and Fifth Graders expand their out-of-school explorations: fourth graders by 3 days study of colonization and an original play; fifth graders engage in problem-solving around caves and crystallography, spending a day a week in a different cave site for each visit.

The Middle School program (sixth, seventh and eighth) encompasses challenge as a key motivation for learning. A week-long wilderness experience in the sixth grade introduces students to hiking, canoeing, and orienteering in a national wilderness area. A look at the geography, economics, natural resources, and history of the state culminates in a visit to the state capitol to conduct interviews with members of the state's house and senate.

Environmental issues at grade seven often combine with a hands-on community project and includes an extended biking trip and camp-out, plus the urban experience in which students work at real jobs in various parts of the city. The culminating experience is a trip to Chicago to study urban issues.

The eighth grade's theme of field ecology includes a 9-day trip to the Great Smokey Mountains, Okefenokee Swamp, and a barrier island for a comparative study of different habitats. Students also spend a week in a 19th Century cabin in St. Genevieve where they research the history of that small Missouri town.

Director Phillips sums up The College School experience this way: "While there is no magic formula for producing a student who is intellectually, emotionally, socially, and physically prepared for today's constantly changing world, our children have countless opportunities for personal as well as academic growth."

THE PROCESS

The College faculty use a team process which they recognize is always in need of nurturing, team building activities and a collective effort to develop "group thinking." Teacher autonomy has been a part of the school's history, yet the ambitious curriculum referenced in program highlights demands a team approach to include academic webbing, field experiences, and the preplanning that must be ongoing. The process, however, evolves out of the school's mission that encompasses experiential, thematic, integrated learning. Teachers spend a lot of time (before school, after school and many weekends) developing the thematic, umbrella topic, and proceeding to integrate as many academic, and fine arts areas that work. Teachers select three themes each year, crossing two grades, until the middle level which crosses three. Writing is integrated throughout every single theme. Assessments also include research, book illustrations, and graphic displays.

Four years ago The College School was invited to join the Danforth Foundation Network on change in the schools, the only private school to be selected. Director Phillips reports that understanding the change process is also a "grieving process" in which they found that it is not easy to challenge the integrity of what you already have for "new things," in spite of the fact that this small school has always been considered by others as a leader in innovation. Together the faculty have progressed through stages of denial, anger, self-examination, and finally to areas of new experimentation. Because they are a part of the Danforth network and committed to dissemination of their learning process, there has been a struggle to document and pull together their findings. There is, for example, a changing vision with parent partnerships playing a more prominent role. Teachers are looking at and changing how they organize. The Faculty Issues Committee sits down with the director at the beginning of the year to plan staff-development priorities and the format/content of weekly faculty meetings that take place after school for 2 hours on a weekly basis. Examples of issues are:

- Children are everyone's responsibility
- How do you make a theme?
- Sharing in math and the communication arts

There is usually a child staffing segment of every meeting. Revisiting their school vision, engaging in positive correspondence (sharing calls or letters written to parents and children) are balanced against tougher issues of sexual harassment and diversity.

In this small school setting that depends so much upon effective teaming, a committee of three to five faculty (always including the team member who may be teamed with the new person) join the director for the hiring process. They collectively screen as a group to determine who will be interviewed. Like each member of the hiring group, the director has one vote. The interviews involve open-ended questions and, whenever possible, the final two candidates are invited to the school to engage in some teaching.

WHAT CAN WE LEARN?

Current research on teaching and learning points to the need for students to be engaged in active learning. Certainly, The College School is an outstanding example of providing countless opportunities for students to experience the world directly, to explore, to research, to synthesize and "try on" the world in an appropriately developmental way. What we can learn is that a vision can be sustained over time while the curriculum (in the hands of an expert staff) evolves and changes to meet the needs of a changing world.

There are professionals in the teaching field who will read this profile and think, "This is not for me! I could never make the commitment of time that is implicit in the autonomy and collective responsibility enjoyed by this staff." There may be other readers, however, who might welcome this challenging environment, recognizing the intrinsic rewards that must be there for so many of the College faculty to reach their "Tenth Year Celebration." Phillips describes these events as celebrations personally designed for the honoree. Not only is there a handsome gift (in the $200 range) for the classroom, but each classroom plans something special, and a lunch, or roast, attended by colleagues. Recently, a 10th year celebrant threatened to "quit if a fuss is made over me." The obliging staff sent flowers to her home and provided a quiet dinner out with her husband.

A shared vision, team-building, shared leadership, and shared decision-making have been a part of The College School since its beginning. The Director's role is that of cheerleader, coach, and keeper of the flame. Beginning on page 40 (Fig. 2.2), we include a representative newsletter from Jan Phillips to the faculty and parents. Parts of the newsletter are also written by parents (Fig. 2.3 beginning on page 42) and occasionally by faculty and students (Fig. 2.4 on page 44); it is far more than an information piece, it provides a written avenue for bonding among the stakeholders. As a Danforth demonstration site, The College School is open to sharing its collaborative processes as well as the teaching approaches, many of which are being adapted in other settings. Certainly, the research of Harvard's Howard Gardner and others who espouse real world experiences outside the classroom supports The College School's efforts.

"Thirty years ago we broke the mold, insisting that students experience and engage in 'real world' problems and challenges. My advice to anyone who values or is interested in developing such a program is . . . to do it. It is absolutely educationally the way to go!"

Jan Phillips, Director, The College School

SCHOOL STATISTICS

The College School
One Newport Place
Webster Groves, Missouri

Director (phone): Jan Phillips 314/962–9355

Number students: 218, prekindergarten through grade 8
Number faculty: 10

FIGURE 2.2. MESSAGE FROM THE DIRECTOR, THE COLLEGE SCHOOL

Message from the Director

 The following article, written by Jan Phillips, was published in the October issue of Education St. Louis, Volume IV, Issue V (1993).

What a great idea for Education St. Louis to focus on failures—or successes from failures... I love it! The idea that failure can be a success story has been a long-standing sentiment at The College School. It was a part of the way we looked at experiments in education thirty years ago when the expression was, "Failure is only a failure if you don't try something else," and "Failure is not a failure if you learn something from it."

Last year at our Alternative Energy Car Demonstration one of the judges was talking to the kids who had designed the various cars and asked, "How many of you found this easy and got your design to work on the first attempt?" Many proud children with smiling faces raised their hands and held them high. Then the judge asked, "How many of you got frustrated or found that your design didn't work and had to redesign your idea?" A few hesitant students raised their hands shoulder high for a second. The speaker continued, "Congratulations. You

are the inventors of the world! Inventors get frustrated. They try ideas that don't work. The exciting thing about inventors is that they keep trying and working through new thoughts and new designs."

Failure has good company! (Check patents, history books, or scientific papers for examples.) Actually, wasn't the discovery of America a failure for the designed mission?

I remember a project that a group of students in a theme on the Mississippi River decided to do. We had read a chapter from Huck Finn and his adventures on the river. This crew wanted to build a raft to float on the river. They looked at various models, talked with a barge pilot and an engineer, and designed a raft using 55-gallon barrels as a base.

They launched the raft on the Meramec River at the Winter Park boat ramp area. It floated magnificently and rode high in the water. But, try as we would, each time the teams of four got on board, the raft flipped upside down! (And,

each crew of the class tried using different strategies.)

Students watched the raft flip upside down, over and over again. Each flip exposed the underside of the raft with its barrels and a small space high enough for one person.

Undaunted, the d gners capitalized on the way t : raft floated and declared the vehicle a one-passenger raft.

Across the ginal underside of the raft, the students painted bold lettering declaring, "This side up!"

Indeed, it's a fine line that separates failure or success.

Another group literally spent hours carefully measuring poster borders for a display. The pencil lines were meticulously measured and drawn at ¾" x 1" x 1" x 1" on the four sides. Photographs, quotes, and illustrations telling about the experience were carefully arranged within the poster's borders.

The day the display was to go up for viewing by the

parents and the rest of the school community, one student decided the borders needed to be a darker line and took a black magic marker to every display poster. The results were striking. Shadowing and covering the carefully plotted pencil borders was a freehand, curly, wavy, crude border that took seconds to produce.

The rest of the class was extremely upset by the quick fix—and let the free-hand artist know it. That day was a dark one for that student. However, in the years that followed, students surveyed the displays to find the best ideas and to locate pitfalls to avoid for their displays. The casually drawn borders have become a great learning source for others — and I always tell how meticulously they were originally measured.

Success or failure? It's all in the way you look at it.

I suspect we as educators need more experience at flipping this two-sided coin. Attitudes and exposures for redirecting and rethinking designs, problems, or solutions give us opportunities to become more creative and better risk-takers in our approaches. It encourages us to look at change.

Flipping failure to success develops even more creative risk-taking qualities in our children. Here's to the failure turnaround!

FIGURE 2.3. MESSAGE FROM A PARENT

Message from a Parent

Submitted by Liz Aurbach (Anne, 6th Grade

When you are new to a place, as we are new to The College School, everything (significant or slight) impresses; some things refreshingly (no styrofoam!), others mystifyingly (a *blanket* permission slip?). As The College School family celebrates 30 years of adventure and achievement, our family is just getting acquainted with the character and culture of the place. To some extent we can't help but compare with our former school. We're learning to say "Roster," not "buzz book;" to sell gift wrap, not Christmas trees; to see you in The Commons, not "by the Office." (Nothing compares with a frozen bandana.) But it's not the lingo that attracts us.

First Impression   We were a small group — just Rick, Jan Phillips, and me — on a guided tour of a secondary school. *Every* classroom we poked our noses into, two or three or more students left their desks to hug Jan. Our "quick" tour took all morning because, as we've come to understand, those College School graduates were embracing something larger than a former teacher.

Open Door   Rick and I had an initial conversation in Jan's office, punctuated by a succession of people, mostly very young ones, popping in to say, *"Hello, Mrs. P.,"* to read a poem, to mention something interesting. This particular 'open door' establishes a spirit of welcome and inclusion and shapes the way folks think about the school. A child who is comfortable dropping in on the Director is likely to understand that she's a valued and valuable member of the community.

Expectations   It's a kindness to tell people what to expect before they jump into something new. Our thanks to teachers and parents who wrote and published *The Middle School Handbook* and *The Parent Handbook*, both well read at our house last summer. Our first day of school was terrifying (but not paralyzing as First Days at new schools can be) and the terror melted fast because all was as you said.

Teachers   We expect teachers to know their subject matter. What's unexpected are teachers whose literacy encompasses Literature and Math, as well as our Environment. They know Aldo Leopold, *and* they know a great place to find crawfish, *and* they'll take you to both.

Backpacks   Not only are camping trips part and parcel of the curriculum (not so elsewhere), this school can outfit a whole class with backpacks, Sierra cups, and stuff sacks. Nevermind orienteering, the ropes course and the wilderness trip (a whole week in a national forest, a solo sleep-out, canoeing, rappelling, and the dirtiest, happiest kid I've ever seen.) Rick is still telling anyone who'll listen, *"Ann came home with a backpack. The whole class got them."*

Displays   All schools have cor-ridor galleries hung with student art and writing. Typically, what goes on the wall *is* the student's complete experience — working with colors and shapes, or with nouns and verbs. Although making a Display at The College School is also an experience grappling with graphics and lan-guage, it is corollary to *the* experience which happened last week in a field or forest. What's astonishing about Displays, whether the quotes are contemplative or comic, is that one after another, they're uni-versally eloquent. We didn't know Ann could write like that (and neither did she). Heretofore, no one had asked her to do it.

The Collage   The effort and organi-zation that goes into this sheaf unfailingly, week after week, is as impressive as it is informative. I assume I'm not the only parent who craves to know more *(more, MORE!)* about what's happening at school. This packet is a happy fix. That the *"Message from the Director"* might be written by someone else is a risky, trusting business (unheard of else-where). It strengthens the collective voice of the school and (until just now) enlightens by articulating new perspectives. Thanks for yielding this space to me! We're delighted to be here. *Happy Anniversary!*

FIGURE 2.4. MESSAGE FROM A STUDENT

Message from a Student

Submitted by Susan Long

Last week, I was excited when Mrs. Phillips asked me to write an article for the *Collage*. I'm in seventh grade and finishing my second year at The College School. Mrs. Phillips wanted to know why I like the Middle School.

I visited The College School the summer before sixth grade, and I liked what I saw. Even though there was a lot of fixing and cleaning going on, the student's displays were creative and fun to look at. I also liked the skeleton of an animal hanging on the ceiling in the Commons. Even though the idea of writing in a journal every two weeks alarmed me a little, I thought this school would be an exciting place to be; and I was right!

Why do I like The College School?

Freedom. We are encouraged to be ourselves and to try different things. We also learn that all of our ideas may not be successful... but that's OK. In sixth grade I was surprised that I could choose some of my own courses. I liked that. This trimester, I am involved in an independent study about Archaeology. I have always wanted to do it, and now I have.

Digging-in. Instead of reading a chapter about a subject like Western Expansion, at The College School we "dig-in" and get our hands dirty. Instead of just reading about Mountain Men and Trappers, reading about their cold nights on the prairie, reading about the buffalo and beaver they ate, *WE* are the Mountain Men struggling to stay warm in a one-sided shelter, eating buffalo burgers, and hiking to rendezvous with the Indians. Talk about digging in!

Classmates and Teachers. I really like the way the middle schoolers are comfortable working on group projects and communicating with each other. In many schools seventh graders would be grouped with seventh graders only, but at our school we have classes with sixth graders and eighth graders which makes it more fun and interesting. I like the way our teachers encourage us to ask questions and do not mind if we disagree.

Field Trips. I love them! Whether we are surviving in the Illinois woods, interrogating state officials in Jefferson City, or braving the six-hour van trips to and from Chicago, I love them! What else can I say? [EDITOR'S NOTE: *Perhaps it's to say that the importance attached to social development is very important during the Middle School years.*]

To make a long story longer, there sure is a lot to like about The College School!

Susan has the perspective of being able to compare us with another school. You'll probably remember her as the girl with an incredible solo singing number at the Variety Show.

Oh, yes, another notable feature is that Susan has registered with Duke University's TIP Talent Search (Talented Identification Program). Susan's ACT test placed her at the top for high scoring participants. Her scores qualified her for a state recognition ceremony; and furthermore, she was invited to the Grand Recognition ceremony on the Duke campus — the top honor given by the talent search program. Well done, Susan!

Jan Phillips

REFERENCES

Abbott, M.G. 1965. "Hierarchical impediments to innovation in educational organizations." *Changes perspectives in educational administration.* Auburn, AL: School of Education, Auburn University, pp. 40–53.

Koehler, Michael D. Education's invisible organization. *American Secondary Education,* Vol. 20, No. 3, 1992, pp. 29–30.

Sergiovanni, T., and R. Starrett. 1993. *Supervision: a redefinition.* New York: McGraw-Hill.

3

THE HIERARCHY AND TEACHER MOTIVATION

Of all the people in our society who should reflect a clear understanding of motivation, teachers and school administrators should be foremost among all of us. They have experienced the frustrations and the fulfillment of meandering through a daily maze of human motivation. Fortunately, it is not uncharted territory, so they also have benefited from the thinking of scores of theorists and the experiences of thousands of practitioners.

Some, however, still struggle with the concept, in much the same way that many still confuse the teaching/learning process. Some teachers have yet to learn that education is only partially a function of teacher behavior; more appropriately, it emphasizes the activities of students. Those who have learned this fact engage students in activities that satisfy their ego and social needs and that promote their interaction with the material to be learned.

Growing numbers of teachers have learned this lesson. Why, then, do so many school systems still regard teacher motivation as something *administrators* do? Consider this administrative myth:

> *Myth Number Five:* "Managerial incentives, control factors, and working conditions have primary influence on the professional behaviors of teachers."

Managerial incentives and other control factors are evident in a wide number of school systems across the country and are elements in the school's overall attempts to motivate teachers.

47

Such school systems recognize the importance of rewarding teachers for their extra effort. They also acknowledge the need to provide a comfortable and relaxing work environment.

Like the misconceptions about teaching, however, such factors often focus on what administrators do and may, in fact, relate more to *their* needs than to the needs of their teachers. Administrators want teachers to abide by school policies and to provide the predictability of behavior that is so important within any organization. They want teachers to participate on committees and develop programs that ostensibly meet the needs of students and staff and that provide high-profile programs within the school community.

They develop reward systems, therefore, that acknowledge the work of teachers. Such extrinsic motivations attempt to influence the professional performance of teachers by giving them merit pay, personal leave days, and air conditioners in the teachers' lounge. These rewards can be marginally successful. Teachers tend to feel a kinship with administrators who provide such "perks."

To be good motivators, however, administrators are well-advised to recognize that such rewards are only "perks" and that, although they do much to strengthen relationships within the school, they do little to stimulate the improved professional performance of teachers. Certainly, all teachers need comfortable and financially rewarding working conditions, but their primary needs relate more to meaningful responsibilities and a sense of competence than to a few extra dollars at the end of the year.

THE FARMER AND THE SEED: A FABLE

Consider the farmer and the seed. All of us would be mighty hungry if farmers rewarded and nurtured seeds *after* they grew. Certainly, young plants require care when they begin to grow, but seeds don't become plants if they fail to receive proper nurturing when first put in the soil. Farmers realize this, so they plant seeds, then care for them by nourishing the soil, watching over them, and removing obstacles to their growth.

They understand the importance of providing the proper environment, and they suffer with their crops when that environment becomes unpredictably harsh or otherwise uncaring. Farmers realize the need to cultivate the environment in which their crops are expected to grow, and they understand, most of all, that any inclination to grow is in the seed—not in the farmer.

They realize that no matter how badly they want the crop to grow, nothing will happen unless the fundamental needs of the seed are satisfied by a nourishing environment. No amount of exhortation or pleading can substitute for a proper environment to promote growth. So it is with motivation. The inclination to grow is in the teachers. They will improve their professional performance only if the school environment promotes such growth—on a daily basis. Merit pay and other incentive programs water the crop at the end of the season, not during the year when nourishment is most needed.

To extend the farmer analogy, consider the school's program of professional growth as it relates to teacher motivation. Many schools that emphasize incentive programs such as merit pay at the end of the year also focus almost exclusively on summative evaluations. They assume that an end-of-the-year evaluation, especially when combined with merit salary increases, will promote improved teacher performance in years to come.

Evaluation is measurement—an assessment of "what is" at any given moment in time. It contains little potential for improving performance, only measuring current performance. Look at it this way. If measurement alone promoted growth, farmers would spend the better part of each day moving from stalk to stalk with a tape measure. Then, when each stalk grew sufficiently, they would reward that growth with fertilizer and water increases, being sure to give the best increases to the stalks that grew the most.

MOTIVATION AND TEACHERS

Fortunately, farmers know better. They cultivate the soil before planting, and then they nourish the soil, tend the plants, and nurture them on a daily basis to promote their growth. They influence the environment so that it satisfies the basic needs of each plant. Good administrators do the same with teachers. They provide a nurturing work environment, and they promote growth by satisfying the fundamental needs of teachers: their needs for recognition, a sense of accomplishment, feelings of autonomy and competence, and increased responsibility.

Extra money and improved working conditions can be complementary motivators. They are effective in creating caring relationships within the school. As Abraham Maslow and Frederick Herzberg stipulated decades ago, however, the daily search for recognition, accomplishment, and responsibility are the higher-order needs of teachers and are the motivators that lead to improved performance and professional growth.

Herzberg went so far as to indicate that the need for money and improved working conditions promote a "participative investment" in teachers, a willingness to meet the minimal expectations of their jobs. In other words, good salary and a nice place to work are sufficient to "motivate" teachers to satisfy their job descriptions. To extend themselves beyond the minimal expectations of their jobs, however, to realize what Herzberg called the "performance investment," they require higher order motivators: recognition, accomplishment, competence, and responsibility.

Myth Number Six: "The growing number of 'burned out' or otherwise intransigent teachers in many of the nation's schools constitutes a serious challenge to school hierarchies to identify improved ways to influence teacher behavior."

This statement is a myth in many schools only because it fails to accommodate the primary motivational needs of teachers. It sustains the focus on the behaviors of administrators as opposed to the needs of the staff. It seems to imply that the administrative hierarchy must do something to teachers to revitalize them, to reaffirm their commitment to the school's normative values. As such, it refocuses on the needs of the hierarchy and assumes that teachers can be controlled by external factors.

Certainly, schools must constantly search for improved ways to influence teacher behavior. Recent theories, however, most of which are consistent with the fundamental principles of motivation, emphasize the importance of exploring the environment for its failure to accommodate the internal needs of the staff. The improvement of behavior, therefore, especially for intransigent teachers, is a function more of system self-analysis than of somehow "changing" teachers.

W. Edwards Deming and Roger Kaufman have been telling us for decades that most of the problems in organizations, including teacher intransigence, are systemic. They result more often from inadequate processes within the system, less often from teacher resistance or incompetence. In fact, Deming has indicated often that up to 90% of all problems within organizations are the fault of the system, not the individuals within it.

Such a position also is consistent with Douglas McGregor's notion that Theory Y administrators trust the fundamental need of teachers to grow personally and professionally. They firmly believe that teachers genuinely want to improve their performance, that all they need is an environment that promotes such growth. When both teacher growth and organizational performance suffer, the experienced administrator looks first for problems within the system itself.

Effective teacher motivation, therefore, considers the impact of the system on teacher behavior. It accepts the evident knowledge that teachers desire a sense of competence, then it looks at the school system to see if it is accommodating that desire. Teachers may be intransigent, therefore, because the system fails to provide for their basic needs, not because teachers are somehow resistant to cooperating with the expectations of the hierarchy.

LOOKING FOR PROBLEMS

Finding motivational problems within the system is relatively easy. Unwilling teachers are readily identified in any school. Centuries of sophisticated pedagogy pale before the uncomplicated good judgment of students, parents, and others in the building when it comes to identifying poor teaching. Everyone in the school community knows the bad teachers. Many even know the uncommitted ones. Why such teachers are uncommitted, however, is more difficult to determine.

The system is responsible to its students and their parents to remediate or to dismiss unwilling and unable teachers. Often, such teachers will respond to some form of intensive evaluation. Uncommitted teachers generally require a different organizational response. The source of their problems is more often in the system than in them. They may respond to increased supervision, but, more often, they require one or more changes in the organization.

Consider some of the possible reasons. School systems sometimes establish policies that stifle teacher creativity or create adversarial relationships with the staff that result in poor attitudes and uncommitted classroom performance. No paradigm in psychological theory provides better insights into such circumstances than Abraham Maslow's Hierarchy of Needs. See Figure 3.1.

FIGURE 3.1. MASLOW'S HIERARCHY OF NEEDS

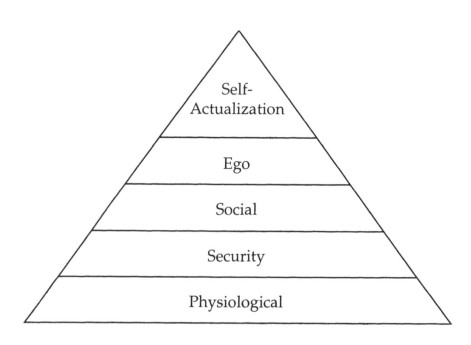

We are reminded that the Hierarchy moves from lower-level needs such as food and drink to higher-order needs such as ego development and self-actualization. Maslow tells us that successively higher needs can't be met until the lower-level needs are satisfied. Imagine, then, one or more teachers unable to move beyond the security level of the hierarchy because of the school's evaluative procedures or the nature of its interpersonal relationships.

According to Maslow, such teachers, because of their preoccupation with security, are unable to satisfy their social and ego needs and will never actualize their potential as teachers, perhaps not even as parents or friends. Such teachers are often perceived by short-sighted administrators as unwilling to commit to the school's normative values or somehow unable to "fit in." What is more likely, however, is the school's inability to satisfy the security needs of the teachers.

In such circumstances, it is administratively expedient to blame the teachers, to depersonalize the staff by regarding them as collectively resistant to change. Unfortunately, it is easier to blame the staff than to engage in the hierarchical self-reflection that explains the impact of the system on teacher behavior. The impact of the system is also reflected in the kinds of planning activities that are evident in many schools.

How often do some administrators identify desirable new programs and implement them without providing the in-service training or the additional planning that is required for the program's success? Sometimes they even introduce such programs as solutions to apparent problems, using the "band-wagon approach" to implement popular trends that may or may not respond to the school's needs. In essence, many of them apply well-conceived solutions to poorly-defined problems.

At that point, how often do some school systems attribute the failure of the program to "teacher resistance" or their inability to master new concepts? Such a predisposition disregards the most basic concepts of motivation. If, like McGregor, we believe that most teachers are sincere in their desire to improve their competencies and sense of autonomy, then our job as administrators is to guarantee the organizational environment that helps them achieve such goals. Appropriate planning is only one element in that environment.

SELF-REFLECTION AND THE HIERARCHY

Supervision in several schools now complements traditional evaluation with activities that promote teacher reflection and self-evaluation. Self-reflection is also important within the administrative hierarchy. It has become so important that just the hint of organizational dysfunction now causes most forward-thinking administrators to look for the nearest mirror to ask themselves what they are doing to contribute to the problem.

In most instances, they are discovering that the dysfunction is a result of system failure, some of which is their fault. Adversarial relationships, low synergy, poor program planning, inadequate supervision, highly centralized decision-making, staff cutbacks, insufficient resources, and a variety of similar situations can influence teacher behavior so that motivation suffers. When such factors cause teacher motivation to focus on security needs, their sense of commitment to organizational purposes and their desire to improve their professional performance suffer.

At that point, incentive programs and other managerial control factors fail to address the fundamental problems within the system, and the school becomes increasingly dysfunctional. Even a well-intentioned analysis of the system's individual parts can fail to identify problems if the school's subsystems are considered in isolation of each other. What is needed by the school's administration is a willingness to "look in the mirror" followed by "system synthesis," a close examination of the interdependency and the mutual interaction of the school's different elements.

This willingness to determine how one subsystem, including the school's administration, may be affecting others within the school is an important initial step in promoting improved teacher motivation. Teachers are especially impressed by administrators who identify problems within the system, some of which have been caused by the hierarchy, and acknowledge them as obstacles to teacher performance.

Their efforts are especially effective when they work with teachers to find ways to eliminate such obstacles in order to promote the organizational environment that enables teachers to satisfy their higher-order needs. Teachers who have satisfied their social and ego needs and find themselves in a school environment that promotes their self-actualization as teachers and persons accept the goals of the organization as consistent with their own and are motivated to help achieve them.

We have learned over the years that morale in any school is highest when teachers can satisfy their own needs as they contribute simultaneously to the normative values of the school. In other words, teachers feel good about themselves and their jobs when their needs are met while they meet the needs of their students. The satisfaction of such needs constitutes the essence of teacher motivation.

Like the farmer, therefore, successful administrators cultivate the school environment, enriching opportunities for teachers and removing obstacles to their personal and professional growth. Good administrators recognize that teachers are already motivated when they enter the building each day. Schools need only provide an environment that cultivates each teacher's natural predisposition to do his or her job as effectively as possible. George Westinghouse Vocational High School in Brooklyn, New York, has chosen to address both teacher and student motivation through a Total Quality Management Process which they have adapted to fit their unique system. It is important to remember that TQM is a continuous improvement process that improves the system (and subsystems) within which people operate. For Westinghouse, the quality process is making a significant difference as our next school profile reveals.

GEORGE WESTINGHOUSE VOCATIONAL HIGH SCHOOL
BROOKLYN, NEW YORK

COLLABORATIVE COMPONENTS

- ◆ Implements a Total Quality Management process in an innercity school, showing dramatic improvement

- ◆ Employs a Quality Steering Committee (volunteers from faculty, students, support staff) as the driving force for change

- ◆ Involves students in decision processes who, in turn, share responsibility for results

- ◆ Gives high priority to staff development and building the learning capacity of all stakeholders

- ◆ Resulting higher student achievement makes this a story worth telling

OVERVIEW

Westinghouse High School in Brooklyn, New York, was a typical innercity high school before the Fall of 1991 when Total Quality Management (TQM) was introduced. Student apathy was evidenced by high dropout rates, high class failure rates, and little excitement about the learning process. Faculty suffered from burnout and a defensiveness resulting from their inability to "reach the students." There were improvement efforts and new programs were introduced, but still the divergent pieces needed a structure and a process to tie it all together.

Assistant principal Franklin Schargel had been introduced to the principles of TQM and the teachings of one of the quality gurus, W. Edwards Deming, before he arrived at

Westinghouse in 1987. The invitation to come to Westinghouse was extended by Schargel's colleague and friend,
principal Louis Rappaport. Together they decided to initiate
a quality continuous improvement process which was, at
that time, gaining attention in other places, including
business and service agencies. The two school leaders formed
a Steering Committee of teachers and administrators and
began training and learning together about quality. Parents
and students would be added in succeeding years.

Training focuses on the techniques and tools of TQM that
include affinity diagrams, histograms, and forced field
analysis, among others. These tools, in turn, provide a
database for benchmarking improvement. The quality
process changes the way people think of schools. Students
are clients, parents are seen as important internal customers;
together, based on real data, decisions are made to improve
learning at Westinghouse.

PROGRAM HIGHLIGHTS

Westinghouse High School celebrated its 75th year in the
1994–95 school year. Beginning in Fall, 1991, the Quality
Steering Committee, now comprised of teachers, administrators, parents, and students, tackled such issues as the high
dropout rate, need for more parent involvement, poor
freshman performance, poor community image, low SAT
scores, and low employee morale. The committee began
weekly meetings, forming Quality Action Teams around an
area of concern. The quality process of plan-do-study-act
ensures that problem-solving uses real data gathering and
that results are measured. For example, in addressing the
dropout problem it was decided to link incoming freshmen
with seniors in a "buddy system." Seniors took the responsibility for planning (and getting feedback) on the mentoring
process. Dropout rates for freshmen began to decrease
immediately. Orientation sessions were instituted for each
grade level. Also, beginning in the Summer of 1992, more
than 500 incoming freshmen participated in a Quality
Academy sponsored by Westinghouse. The Academy

emphasized life-long learning, as well as the principles of quality. It was jointly taught by faculty and students who had completed the quality training for the Steering Committee.

Many, many changes have occurred at Westinghouse as the learning environment has improved for all who work and learn there. Teachers bend union rules and attend subcommittee (action team) meetings twice a week which are scheduled at 7:15 AM and 2:15 PM to meet individual needs. Regular faculty meetings have a staff development component which means that the formal "meeting business" is now distributed before the meetings in memorandum form. Over a 2-year period, union grievances have dropped from 29 to 2.

A poignant example of changing community image occurred when assistant principal Schargel met with the administration of Brooklyn Polytechnical University which sits across the street from Westinghouse. He met to ask why the university would not accept even a few of the most talented seniors at Westinghouse and learned that the SAT scores of the highest achievers were too low. It was also pointed out that the verbal communication skills of Westinghouse graduates were very poor compared to the University's entrance expectations. Schargel explained that they could do something about improving speech skills, but no Westinghouse student could afford Princeton Review, or any other SAT preparation course. Together, the University and the high school developed a plan for Polytech students to tutor Westinghouse students in preparation for SAT's. Later, in gathering data to benchmark the progress, they discovered a need and added a PSAT awareness session in the junior year. Speech classes, components of the English program, were also instituted. As a result of the first year of tutoring, the number of seniors taking the SAT rose from 26 to 73. Today, Polytech has created four $18,000 scholarships to be awarded to graduating Westinghouse seniors and the tech library is open to the high school students. SAT scores are continuing to rise.

THE PROCESS

Total Quality Management (TQM) or Total Quality Improvement (TQI) depends on a cyclical process that is ongoing (rather than a linear process with a beginning, middle, and end). In 1939, Dr. William Shewhart conceived a four-step plan called the P-D-C-A (Plan-Do-Check-Act). This was later changed by W. Edwards Deming to P-D-S-A (Plan-Do-Study-Act). The vast body of literature on Total Quality Management reveals that all of its adherents espouse such a four-part process.

Quality is a continuous and long-term undertaking. It is not a "program" that can be learned and implemented after a period of intensive training. It works only when it is well thought-out and adapted to the specific organization. Key to implementation is continuous training. At Westinghouse a quality coordinator was designated who, in turn, could train others at the school. In the early stages, as many faculty as possible were sent to corporate training sessions at, e.g., IBM, Xerox. Limited budget remains one of the constraints in sustaining the process.

As TQM developed at Westinghouse, collaborative leadership grew as shared decision-making replaced the old autocratic system. Today, the Quality Steering Committee runs the school. Anyone (including students) who wants to be a part of the process meets every Thursday at 7:15 AM and again at 2:15 PM that same day. The committee builds its own agenda; task forces and action plans grow out of the group decisions. One Thursday, the committee agenda included items on building security and rewards for students. The rewards issue was actually a debriefing of the third annual Quality Student Recognition Ceremony. Students received recognition if they averaged 80% and above in their academic program or 85% and above in their work experience program. This year's ceremony was attended by 425 people. This is especially significant considering that the majority of the students travel up to 2 hours on public transportation to reach their school. Students proudly pointed to their use of the quality process to improve the award ceremony's attendance each year. Year one, letters were sent home. Year two, a tear-off RSVP was added to the letter. This year, using the improvement process to double the attendance, they sent the letter with the RSVP and added personal phone invitations from the student committee. Students explain that "debriefing" is an integral part of their continuous improvement process.

Improving communication is the biggest challenge according to principal Lewis Rappaport. The Steering Committee recently initiated a newsletter entitled, *Our House.* The principal also employs an "off-the-record" segment at the close of every Steering Committee meeting where anyone can discuss any problem or concern. This practice was adapted from the U.S. Navy's practice of "Talk with the Captain." Another worry is sustaining the remarkable progress that has occurred at Westinghouse under TQM. In the first year, the dropout rate decreased dramatically to 2.1%. In year four, it is up to 4.4%, still a very low rate compared to other New York City Schools, and an expected increase according to research on organizational change.

Clearly, this process is making a difference at Westinghouse in a way that directly impacts student learning. Many schools across the country are being introduced to quality improvement; they can learn from the Westinghouse experience. In 1994, assistant principal Franklin Schargel published a book, *Transforming Education Through Total Quality Management: A Practitioner's Guide,* about Westinghouse's TQM experience.

WHAT CAN WE LEARN?

Using the TQM quality process, the school culture of Westinghouse has changed significantly. TQM, if successfully adapted, places responsibility for learning with the students. The quality movement, whose gurus include Deming, Juran, Scholte, and others, is increasingly adapted to school settings. For the skeptics who insist that education has nothing to learn from business, it is good to remember that schools are organizations too. Systems thinking, as Peter

Senge writes in his classic 1990 book, *The Fifth Discipline,* is needed in every organization. Conversely, schools should not be the only learning community. Leaders, in this case the principal and assistant principal, will tell you that the process "flattens the hierarchy" as it develops leadership among the many stakeholders who engage in the process.

Rappaport and Schargel of Westinghouse maintain that for any quality implementation to succeed, the following basic tenets must be in place:

+ There must be a commitment of support and involvement from the administration.

+ The school must develop and work from a vision statement.

+ A Total Quality Coordinator (or similar position) must be appointed.

+ A Steering Committee must be set up.

+ Everyone involved must read, read, read (about quality)!

It is also important to remind ourselves that the quality movement is not a program, but a process of continuous improvement. Schools that have successfully embraced TQM find that it integrates the learning components around the school vision. Teachers and students are involved in both the decision-making and measuring processes that are a part of TQM. Training and continuous professional development are integral to its success.

School Statistics

George Westinghouse Vocational Technical High School
105 Johnson Street
Brooklyn, NY 11201

Grades: 9–12
Number of students: 1200

Principal: Lewis Rappaport
Phone: 718/625–6130

REFERENCES

Deming, W. Edwards, quoted in Peter Senge. 1990. "The leader's new work: building a learning organization." *Sloan Management Review*, vol. 22, p. 7.

Herzberg, Frederick. 1966. *Work and the Nature of Man*. New York: World Publishing.

Kaufman, Roger. 1972. *Educational System Planning*. Englewood Cliffs, NJ: Prentice-Hall.

Maslow, Abraham. 1954. *Motivation and Personality*. New York: Harper and Row.

McGregor, Douglas. 1960. *The Human Side of Enterprise*. New York: McGraw-Hill.

4

DECENTRALIZING ADMINISTRATIVE DECISIONS

Consider the fact that education is one of only a few licensed careers governed almost exclusively by lay persons. Such governance may be appropriate, given the local community's financial generosity and cultural expectations of its schools. One can't help but wonder, however, at the implications such governance has on the vested interests of those who manage the schools and on the processes they choose to make decisions.

We are reminded of a question asked earlier in this book: "Who are the clients of our school systems?" If the primary clients are parents, then those of us who work in school systems must be considered employees of the local community, and our decisions must conform to parental expectations. If the primary clients are students, however, then we must be regarded as experts hired by parents to exercise autonomous and professional judgment as we develop and deliver the school's educational programs.

The distinction extends even further. If the primary clients are parents, then school personnel must make at least some decisions that curry the favor of influential citizens. If the primary clients are students, then school personnel are liberated to use their professional expertise to focus decisions on the normative values of the school, some of which may at times may conflict with community expectations.

Obviously, such a circumstance involves a fundamental conflict. On the one hand, trained professionals favor a decisional framework that focuses exclusively on the needs of students, one that constantly promotes the professional growth of teachers and revitalizes the school's educational programs. On the other hand, the world of reality suggests that school decision-makers satisfy the expectations of local parents, the source from which all financial blessings flow.

WHAT ARE THE IMPLICATIONS?

Unfortunately, the implications of some schools' inability to resolve this conflict have resulted in traditional patterns of administrative behavior that may actually interfere with the school's ability to satisfy the needs of the student-as-client. Consider, for example, the requirement that school leaders receive certification in educational administration in order to enter the school hierarchy. Such a requirement is expected equally of district superintendents and individual department heads, persons whose actual contact with students ranges from marginal to frequent.

One might expect a decreasing focus on actual classroom issues as one moves up the pyramid illustrated in Figure 4.1. Superintendents, for example, would be expected to focus on the allocation of budget and personnel and a whole range of legal and organizational issues, while department heads would be expected to provide leadership involving classroom issues and the professional growth needs of staff.

Our discussions with school personnel, however, indicate that the focus on administrative certification, when combined with the nature of administrative and supervisory tasks, results in a primary focus on managerial issues for department heads as well as superintendents. Budget, monthly reports, policy considerations, building and district meetings, staff evaluation, and personnel issues often interfere with the department head's ability to "get into the classroom" and assist with the ongoing professional growth of teachers and the improvement of instructional programs.

FIGURE 4.1. FOCUS ON CLASSROOM ISSUES

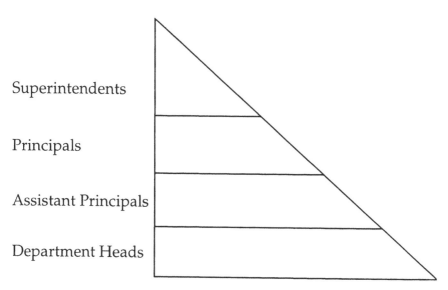

Superintendents

Principals

Assistant Principals

Department Heads

Teachers and the Instructional Program

A frequent result is a circumstance that looks something like the illustration in Figure 4.2. This "L Factor" reflects an administrative focus on managerial issues and suggests the inability of department heads to work closely with teachers on the issues which most directly affect students. It also indicates the inability of teachers, because of their absence of administrative certification, to exercise decisional authority in areas that remain the purview of principals, assistant principals, and department heads.

The administrative certification of department heads only marginally promotes their knowledge of curriculum and instruction, and it results in the predispositions of many to focus on managerial issues. Conversely, the absence of such certification for classroom teachers serves to disengage them from the managerial process, which includes curricular and instructional issues. To quote a popular Broadway lyric: "'Tis a puzzlement!'"

FIGURE 4.2. THE "L FACTOR"

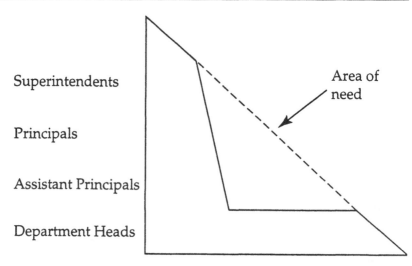

Superintendents

Principals

Assistant Principals

Department Heads

Area of need

Teachers and the Instructional Program

But the problem continues. This disenfranchisement of teachers wastes the expert power they might otherwise bring to curricular and instructional decisions. It also burdens department heads and other administrators with the intimidating responsibility of making all the significant curricular and instructional decisions and of periodically evaluating classroom teachers, many of whom are the real experts in the building.

Mike, on e of the authors of this book, is reminded of one of his first administrative experiences. As a fledgling administrator, he was scheduled to visit the classroom of a former departmental colleague and conduct her triennial evaluation. A veteran of some 30 years experience, she was an acknowledged expert in her field and reportedly one of the best teachers in the district. Fortunately, Mike realized at the time that his 8 years experience as an educator had not prepared him for the task of evaluating a teacher who was unmistakably his superior in the classroom. So he checked "superior" on every category on the evaluation sheet. He thus escaped the experience with only minor bumps and bruises but wonders, to this day, how long she laughed at his dilemma.

The task of having all the answers in an evaluative situation is, indeed, a dilemma for any fair-thinking administrator, young or old. It is made additionally difficult by certification requirements that relate only marginally to classroom instruction and traditions that exclude teachers from ongoing decision-making in the school.

THE TEACHER AS CODEPENDENT

Hierarchical organization has been repeatedly criticized in much of the literature for this exclusion of teachers from school decision-making. What is worse is the impression that is fostered by such exclusion. As Professor Victor Thompson said almost 30 years ago: "The impression is that occupants of hierarchical positions are, of all people in the organization, the ablest, the most industrious, the most indispensable, the most loyal, the most reliable," and the like.

People in nonhierarchical positions, then, necessarily must be perceived at times as *less* indispensable, *less* reliable, and *less* able. Such perceptions are inherent in some schools' relationships and are perpetuated by teachers themselves, an indication of what could be considered their codependency. Codependents are defined as persons who are "currently in a love or marriage relationship with an addict . . . and/or grew up in an emotionally repressive circumstance." (Schaef 1987, p. 29)

Douglas McGregor (1969) and Chris Argyris (1964) presented widely accepted and well-researched positions regarding the repressive characteristics of hierarchical organization. Their positions still constitute the philosophical foundations for the study of educational leadership in most university graduate programs. Lesser known studies have affirmed their positions. In 1967, Grimes observed that employees who perceive their organizations as rigidly hierarchical will experience greater alienation than those who do not have such perceptions.

About the same time, Aiken and Hage (1966) observed that hierarchies are likely to induce worker alienation. And just a few years earlier, Abbott (1965) postulated that hierarchical organization and the tendency of administrators to maintain their status within it accounted, to a large extent, for education's inability to change. Fortunately, some of this is changing, a phenomenon reflected in the program cited at the conclusion of this chapter and in the other chapters of this book.

THE SEARCH FOR STATUS AND TEACHER BURNOUT

In many other schools, however, what changes did occur rarely grew beyond trends and almost never established themselves in the nation's schools. Furthermore, many teachers "enable" what Abbott described as administrative "status charades." Specific examples include the deference that teachers give administrators and the tendency of teachers to seek increased status within the educational community by leaving the classroom.

Perhaps the most evident behavior, however, and the one most consistent with codependency, is the tendency of some teachers to be overburdened and tired—"burned out." Opportunities for self-revitalization are rare among persons who seek constantly to make themselves indispensable to others—to do whatever is necessary to be liked and accepted.

Teachers tend, therefore, to be overworked and to find personal and professional satisfaction in the perceptions of others. They are dependent upon an external reward system, for example, that is found in traditional programs of teacher evaluation. Their resultant tendency to be self-sacrificing not only "burns them out" but affirms the hierarchy's expectations of control. Their codependency, therefore, diminishes their own growth toward autonomy and enhances the power of the system that inhibits that growth.

THE CONTRADICTION OF CARING

This self-sacrificing and caring attitude of teachers, as valuable as it may be during their work with children, is also an impediment to change. As a characteristic of codependency, it is one of the reasons why repressors are viewed negatively and codependents are viewed positively. Their caring reflects a selflessness that is often applauded—but that continues to enable repression. Teachers are applauded for their dedication and selfless commitment to students: "Sure, I'll do it." "What's one more?" "I'm not in it for the money!" "The kids come first!"

Of interest, however, are the findings of Chris Argyris (1960) that teachers in strong hierarchical organizations want two things: to earn good money and to be left alone. He discovered that many of them actually *chose* alienation over active involvement in the school. The "We/They" dichotomy that characterizes the teachers' relationships with school administrators serves to underscore their alienation.

This is not to say that the caring attitudes of teachers are facades. They are genuine characteristics and worthy of the applause they receive from parents and other segments of society. The selflessness they express, however, affirms not only the good intentions of the teacher but the intransigence of schools. Their willingness to "go along" perpetuates organizational patterns in many schools and further inhibits needed change.

The teacher-as-codependent, therefore, has contributed as much as anyone else to the continuation of hierarchical decision-making. Ironically, it is a mode of school organization that often fails to incorporate into planning activities the technical competence of the school's most knowledgeable people—the teachers. Like all codependents, therefore, teachers are the partners as well as the victims of the systems that inhibit them.

Fortunately, current collaborative models, many of which are included in this book, are changing traditional hierarchical relationships in schools. Classroom observation and teacher evaluation have changed dramatically in some schools. Collaborative planning models are growing daily. Unfortunately, such schools are still a minority, and schools generally, especially in large systems, continues to depend on the hierarchy for organization and decision-making.

OLD HABITS DIE HARD

That hierarchical decision-making is firmly established in many of the nation's schools is not surprising. Traditional models of decision-making persist in most of the nation's schools. They are as old as the earliest models of organization, and inherent in well-established, if misguided, philosophical principles:

> *Myth Number Seven:* "The quantity and quality of the decisions one makes in the organization determine the degree of his or her power."

The behaviors of many school administrators and businesspersons reflect their apparent belief of this statement. Tradition favors the dynamic leader who commands the respect of his or her subordinates by making quick and forceful decisions about the operation of the system. As Frederick Taylor indicated 100 years ago in his *Principles of Scientific Management:* "Managers manage and workers work." Such is the destiny of the great leader.

Many decades later, however, Daniel Griffiths postulated that the person who controls the decisional processes within the organization and who makes the fewest terminal decisions is the most powerful and the best liked. Experience has proven him to be correct, and the many models of collaborative planning activity in some of the nation's schools are evidence of the validity of his observation.

To revisit one of Mike's earliest administrative experiences, he was happy indeed when he finally incorporated Griffiths' principle into his administrative behavior. He realized that he didn't have to be responsible for telling a superior teacher what was right or wrong with her teaching. Instead, he learned to ask the questions that promoted her self-reflection; he controlled the process by which she made decisions about her teaching.

She and others in the department liked him because he provided the kind of assistance that promoted good teaching, and they gave him the power to influence their teaching and their thinking about departmental activities. Good administrators learn that the colleague group is the only consistently reliable source of power in the organization. The district and the board of education may invest authority in the administration, but the power to use that authority effectively derives from colleagues and from certain others in the school community.

THE INNER CIRCLE SYNDROME

One final consideration warrants mention. Normally, the substantive decisions in any school are made by the building's principal and assistant principals, the major players in the school's "inner circle." To the extent that they control the building's information flow and make the decisions that affect the lives of just about everyone in the school, membership in the inner circle is desirable, and it becomes a goal for aspiring administrators.

Everyone wants to be a part of the "inner circle." It's human nature. No matter how useless or mundane the activity, it's the inner circle, that very selective and prestigious organizational "club" that awards the most status to its members. The problem is, the inner circle usually deals with issues that are *not* useless and mundane, but critically important to the needs of students and teachers.

If teachers are fortunate enough to become administrators in the building and actually achieve membership in the inner circle, they tend to maintain its traditional way of making decisions. This, too, is a problem because it precludes the input of those others in the building who have the technical expertise to improve the quality of the school's decisions. Membership in the school's hierarchy, then, tends to be desirable *for many of the wrong reasons.*

WHO, THEN, IS THE SCHOOL'S INSTRUCTIONAL LEADER?

Much of the literature would have us believe that the principal is the school's instructional leader. As the superintendent is expected to set the tone for the district, the principal is expected to maintain the vision for the school. And we all know that visions are good. Someone has to have them. In fact, everyone has to have them if an organization is to be successful. The Bible taught us centuries ago that visions experienced by only one or two people can provoke suspicion and misunderstanding, even occasional conflict.

They are most effective when they involve a shared experience, a revelation that is seen and accepted by everyone. The principal's job may be to pronounce the revelation and to help sustain its vision, but its creation requires a process that involves everyone. Only then does a vision illuminate the school's fundamental purposes and promote the shared commitment so necessary to achieve them.

The principal, then, is only one element in the school's focus on its vision. Certainly, he or she is a key element, but the process of creating and proclaiming the central insight that guides a school through its daily responsibility of educating children is an experience shared by everyone. This is the essence of collaboration, to coalesce the broad range of skills that operate in every school in order to develop and sustain a vision, then to cooperate to assure its achievement.

Educators are mistaken, then, to identify the principal as the school's educational leader. Schools are blessed with a broad spectrum of educational leaders, requiring only the opportunity to share their expertise about curriculum and instruction in order to realize their shared vision. The principal's job, therefore, is not to be the school's instructional leader, but to be a leader of instructional leaders, all of whom maintain the school's vision. The Hawthorne School in Seattle, Washington, began with one principal's vision, but evolved in a vision shared not only by the principal and teachers, but the entire community it serves.

HAWTHORNE ELEMENTARY SCHOOL
SEATTLE, WASHINGTON

COLLABORATIVE COMPONENTS

- Builds on a model of relationships and cooperation
- Integrates the broad community as essential to the school's mission
- Supports an active and ongoing partnership between parents and school
- Holds to core values that are sustained by all involved with the school
- Implements a mission that ensures success for all children, particularly those from ethnic minority groups not previously achieving as well as other groups
- Serves as demonstration school for other educators
- Mails every parent an "academic warranty" that their child will be at or above grade level by the time they reach fifth grade

OVERVIEW

Hawthorne Elementary School in the Rainier Valley of Seattle is one school in the 43,000-student district that reopened to a new vision of educating urban children in 1989. The original school, built in 1909, served the city's changing populations—Italian, Asian, African American—before closing in 1979 when it was deemed unsafe.

John Morefield, who began his 30-year career in Seattle public schools as a high school counselor, asked the support of his district Superintendent to create a school that would ensure the success of all children, particularly those from ethnic minority groups not previously achieving as well as other groups. As Hawthorne's principal, he views himself as a strong, collaborative leader; strong in the sense that he will not negotiate on values, and collaborative in the sense that he and all faculty must be free to take risks, to work through conflict, to negotiate opinions and preferences. Together, holding to their set of common educational beliefs, they created the "Hawthorne Way" which, in the intervening years, has met with astounding success.

Those core beliefs are:

+ All children can and will learn.
+ Schools have the paramount duty to ensure that students learn.
+ Students will be successful when there is an active and ongoing partnership between parents and school.
+ The self-fulfilling prophecy is at work in learning. There is a direct relationship between educators' expectations and student achievement.
+ Equity and excellence must go hand in hand.

PROGRAM HIGHLIGHTS

The new Hawthorne School stands at the top of the ridge overlooking Seattle's Rainier Valley. Its opening in 1989 signaled a new beginning; the original Hawthorne building had been closed 10 years earlier. With its rebirth with principal John Morefield, a group of parents and educators have attempted to create a school that guarantees success for all its students. While they don't claim to have all the pieces of this complex puzzle, after pulling ideas from research on effective practices and effective schools, and after traveling throughout the country visiting schools that have been recognized for outstanding practices, Morefield and his staff have identified and are implementing 12 essential characteristics of a school that works for all children:

1. **Strong leadership.** As Roland Barth in his book, *Run School Run*, pointed out, "Show me a good school and I will show you a good principal." Morefield points out that in addition to an inspired, entrepreneurial principal, effective schools need shared leadership, both formal and informal. At Hawthorne that leadership is shared among staff, parents, students and the community. Examples follow of parents and community members providing ongoing support and, most importantly, the shared responsibility for each child's success.

2. **Unity of Purpose.** Purpose, vision, and core values must be known and shared by all adults and children in the school. Commenting in his journal while traveling across the country visiting schools he hoped would expand his knowledge of what works in successful schools, Morefield recorded his disappointment in one: "There is no school purpose or vision outside of the principal's head." Collaborative leaders work to create new ways, both real and symbolic, to keep the dream alive day in and day out.

3. **Nurturing Environment.** Hawthorne's approach to nurturing is to replace the current American adherence to the northern European model of schooling, based on competition among individuals, with a model that reflects the dominant ethic of many peoples of color, cooperation, and relationship. In the latter model, all the stakeholders work together for the success of every child in lieu of the first which rewards winners, even though significant numbers may fail. At Hawthorne, every effort is made to develop and sustain an environment that surrounds the children with warmth, love, affection, and affirmation to thrive.

4. **Adult Responsibility.** At Hawthorne, all children are the responsibility of all the adults. The cultural emphasis is on "we" and "ours." Hawthorne's "Mom" Wilson, a retired teacher who serves as the volunteer coordinator, is one important leader who makes certain that no child falls

through the cracks. She may be greeting each child at the beginning of each day as they get off the bus, overseeing the food and clothing assistance programs, or guiding one of the 120 members of a local Rotary Club who come to tutor or take fifth graders on camping trips. Members of the community, parents, and teachers all work together to deliver on the "academic warranty." This is a community of learners where students know that all adults share concern for them. The focus is always on learning.

5. Firm and Fair Discipline. Faculty reached consensus that a schoolwide discipline structure was needed, both in philosophy and practice, that is firm, fair, consistent, and positive. In many urban schools, race or socioeconomic status are used as silent excuses to disregard the need for a safe, orderly environment. "Our children come from dysfunctional homes," or "Poor, child, we really can't expect more," are not a part of the "Hawthorne way." Staff work together to monitor and support each other. It is acknowledged that adults must be clear and consistent about discipline. Students pledge to uphold The Hawthorne Way:

"We come to school to learn and do our best."

1. We solve problems in a helpful way. Fighting and hurting others is not allowed.
2. We listen to and follow the directions of adults at school.
3. We use proper names and show respect to everyone.
4. We stay on task and complete work.
5. We respect school and personal property.
6. We walk in the building. Our actions are safe at school.
7. We eat treats only at appropriate times. Gum and toys are not allowed during school hours.

6. High Expectations. Research on urban schooling indicates that the number one problem of low achievement is low expectations. Although most teachers will respond that they believe "all children can learn," there is a silent tag to that claim which states that "not all children are educable." To raise expectations teachers may have to unlearn the belief that IQ is innate, fixed, and distributed along a bell-curve continuum. It is Morefield's contention that the bell curve can no longer serve as an operational value. Nor can the belief that in any classroom there is a certain percentage of gifted, average, and at-risk students. These operational values must be replaced with the belief that there is incredible potential in all children. The legacy of racism, including phrases like "culturally deprived," must be shed. When children of color are seen as different (rather than deficient), only then can high expectations be realized.

7. Dedicated Teachers. The teachers' union collaborated with the District in making the Hawthorne demonstration school a reality. Over 125 teachers applied for the 24 available positions in the first year. In a portraiture written by a Hawthorne teacher, Ramona Curtis, she recounts:

> I am used to working hard. I am used to coming early and staying late, but at Hawthorne we ALL do! It is the norm. . . . We have chosen to come to Hawthorne, we believe that teaching is a calling, not only a job. We want to be a part of this Hawthorne, to help create the Hawthorne way. . . . I am not an oddity. Long after I leave John is still at school or out in the community ever expanding the network of people who care, who will make a difference.

Hawthorne's teachers reflect and share their principal's passion and belief that teaching is a "decision of the heart" accompanied by a deeply held commitment to social justice.

8. Multicultural Curriculum. Recognizing that the United States is the most diverse country in the world, and that Hawthorne itself is a rainbow of cultures (38% white,

36% African-American, 24% Asian, with Latino and Native American children making up the remaining 2%) a multicultural curriculum is integrated throughout the instructional program. Most important, in the daily life of the school, is its mission of being culturally friendly. Different cultures are valued, recognized, and celebrated.

9. Outstanding Instructional Practices. As pointed out earlier, both the principal and faculty have charged themselves with implementing the best instructional practices identified by research. For Hawthorne, this means abandoning practices like tracking which may make teaching easier, but interferes with the outcome of academic success for every child. Also out are the textbook-imposed levels of the linear, lockstep curriculum, and pull-out teaching. "In" are integrated curricular content using interdisciplinary and thematic approaches. Multiple teaching strategies accommodate students' multiple learning styles. Whole language approaches and developmentally appropriate instruction are explored and evaluated. The demands on teachers, that teachers place upon themselves, are great. The task is formidable and certainly not for the fainthearted. Supporting best practice is the creative and innovative use of technology. School-based governance that includes real shared decision-making and empowerment of all adults has been in place since the beginning.

10. Parent Involvement. It's not only encouraged, it is expected, because the research shows that parent involvement is essential to ensuring all children's success. At Hawthorne, where there is a full-time volunteer coordinator of volunteers, there is a special room with coffee and chairs to greet all who come to help, including parents. In addition to the friendly environment, activities are planned that include sending invitations, making phone calls, arranging car pools, providing child care and offering affirmation and accolades genuinely and often. Everything is done to highlight the importance of the home-school partnership and its role in the daily life of the school. Hawthorne's families are representative of the broad spectrum of socioeconomic status (one of two students receive free lunch), and single parent homes. All Hawthorne parents are expected to play their role in the partnership.

11. Mental Health Approach. Concerted team efforts that are interdisciplinary and interagency address the many problems and social issues that effect children's learning. Drawing upon the research of psychologist James Comer, Hawthorne faculty seek community assistance in meeting the emotional and psychological needs of the children that arise out of poverty, child abuse, substance abuse, and other social issues. There is recognition that for years classroom teachers were expected to be part-time counselors, social workers, and parents. In the past, when families were more intact, churches stronger, and neighborhoods more inclusive, a teacher could handle a few such demands. Today, a teacher's time, energy, and expertise must be free to focus on the teaching/learning processes.

12. Attractive School Environment. With declining public school funding support, which is most visible in urban settings, are decaying, poorly maintained, unsafe schools. Considering that increasing numbers of children are living in unsafe home environments, it is imperative that school be safe, clean, and attractive. Hawthorne is fortunate to be a "new school building"; in recreating schools that will work for every child, school buildings of whatever age must symbolize the values we place on educating our most important natural resources, our children.

THE PROCESS

There is no question that the success of the new Hawthorne School is intertwined with an admired, dedicated, determined principal, John Morefield. A poster in his office depicts a koala bear holding on to a tree for dear life. The caption reads, "Sometimes you just have to go out on a limb." According to teacher Ramona Curtis, the story of Hawthorne is this principal going out on a limb and inviting others to join him in the adventure. A staff member is quoted as saying what many feel, "I would never work these hours, these days for anyone else!"

Typical of faculties committed to achieving a shared vision, all sorts of shared decisions must be made. The first years have been termed (in Maslow's hierarchy) the "survival years." They met in large groups and small groups throughout the summer. The "what if" committee looking at scheduling proposed, what if we could make a new model, big blocks of noninterrupted classroom time. Other comments and concerns were voiced: "There has to be a better way. We said no pull-outs. We must end disporportionality. Shall we keep our classes for 2 years? What, only one entrance from the playground for 400 kids! Who designed this building, not educators!"

Now, almost 6 years have passed since the beginning of The Hawthorne Way. The initial stress has lessened, although there are still frequent late night dinners for staff and many weekends, plus off-time are devoted to planning and problem-solving. What makes this collaboration different from other schools, according to the teachers, is the absolute belief in the core values. All adults believe (and act accordingly) that learning will take place and that all children will succeed academically. There is a written guarantee mailed to all parents that students coming into Hawthorne in Kindergarten will be at or above grade level at the end of fifth grade. An academic warranty!

WHAT CAN WE LEARN?

There is an growing concern in urban America that is seldom publicly discussed. Can public education survive if the current success rate (student achievement) continues? State legislatures across the country are debating "voucher" issues, with some authorizing learning zones and passing charter school legislation. There is even a growing conviction among organizational development theorists that there has been enough of "trying to fix the system" and only a new system can hope to prepare the educated citizenry needed in American in the 21st century. Within this context, Hawthorne school stands as a model for developing a "new system" of public education.

The Hawthorne Way, some will point out, may not be easily replicated. Visionary leaders, new principals entering established schools, do not have the luxury of creating and "inviting those who share the vision" to join in creating a new system. Changing mental models and existing paradigms of how children learn in schools that have languished with the status quo is a task that some system critics say is impossible, considering what is known about the change process. John Morefield will say that it was his outrage at what was happening to students of color in Seattle that propelled him to engage a faculty, parents and community to make a difference and to make high expectations a reality.

Whether or not Hawthorne remains one of a few or becomes the norm in urban America depends, of course, on many societal factors. But mostly, more importantly, it depends on the leadership of educators who will say, "enough fixing!" Through research we know the structures, the best practices, the collaboration processes and the expectation factors needed for all children to achieve at high levels. Do we have the courage and determination? Do we share the outrage!

SCHOOL STATISTICS

Hawthorne School
4100 39th Avenue South
Seattle, WA 98110

Grades: Kindergarten through 5
Number of students: 480

Principal: John Morefield
Phone: 206/ 281–6664

REFERENCES

Abbott, M. 1965. Hierarchical impediments to innovation in educational organizations. *Changed perspectives in educational administration.* Auburn, AL: Auburn University, pp. 44–47.

Aiken, M., and Hage, J. 1966. Organizational alienation: a comparative analysis. *American Sociological Review.* 31:499.

Argyris, C. 1960. Individual actualization in complex organizations. *Mental Hygiene.* 44(2): 226–237.

Grimes, M.G. 1967. Bureaucracy and personality: the effect of perceived work environment on social integration and alienation. Masters thesis, University of Texas.

Griffiths, D.E. 1959. *Administrative theory.* Englewood Cliffs, NJ: Prentice Hall.

McGregor, D. 1960. *The human side of enterprise.* New York: McGraw-Hill.

Schaef, A.W. 1987. *When society becomes an addict.* New York: Harper and Row.

Thompson, V.A. 1965. Bureaucracy and innovation. *Administrative Science Quarterly.* Vol. 10, No. 1, 1–20.

Parts of this chapter were reprinted with permission of the Helen Dwight Reid Educational Foundation from Koehler, M. "The Teacher as Codependent." *The Clearing House*, Vol. 65, Sept./Oct. 1991, pp. 9–10, published by Heldref Publications, 1319 18th St., NW, Washington, DC 20036–1802.

5

COLLABORATION AND THE PROFESSIONAL GROWTH PROGRAM

Educational supervision has reached a pivotal stage in its evolution. Consistent with the theories of early scientists, it has adapted to its environmental circumstances to ensure the continued survival of its species. In fact, traditional philosophies of supervision, specifically, elements of classroom observation, have adapted to changing environmental expectations so successfully that the earliest forms of professional growth in schools have persisted for the past several decades. Traditional forms of educational supervision are alive and well in schools across the country. The question is: Whose survival are they guaranteeing?

That administrators seem to be the primary beneficiaries of professional growth programs in many of the nation's schools is the main reason why the evolution of educational supervision is at such a pivotal stage. Teacher evaluation, the central, and often the exclusive, element in professional growth, does as much to enhance administrative authority as to influence the competencies of teachers or to improve the learning experiences of students. Look at it this way: teacher evaluation in many schools has become little more than documenting something we can't really prove, about someone we don't really know, to someone who really doesn't care.

This is tragicomedy in its purest sense. As characterized in the nation's media, the antics of school systems regarding decreased reading scores and increased violence have become both laughable and tragic. Even the increased awareness of the situation among teachers and parents has done little to change it. It seems that education has become amazingly efficient at achieving the ineffective. Peter Drucker once said, "There is nothing so useless as doing efficiently that which should not be done at all."

THE WILLINGNESS TO CHANGE

What education has been doing to promote teacher growth, in Drucker's words, "should not be done at all." Observational checklists, for example, are models of efficiency, but they usually fail to mirror teacher performance, or give the teacher a clear look at what actually happened during the class in order to promote self-reflection. Another example involves the hierarchical relationships in schools that almost always give administrators ownership of teacher evaluations.

In essence, if I tell you what is right or wrong with your teaching, I own the evaluation. If you tell me what is right or wrong with your teaching, you own the evaluation. Fortunately, many schools across the country, one of which is included in this chapter, have developed supervision programs that promote teacher ownership of evaluations. They have discovered that teacher ownership results in a more obvious commitment to improvement and to improved learning for students.

Woodrow Wilson explained years ago that judgment should provide light, not heat. President Wilson would be pleased to see that many schools today are using teacher observation as beacons, not blast furnaces. Positive change is evident in such programs. Before we look at the specific programs within the next few pages, let's first acknowledge that they all organize teacher observation around five fundamental questions.

FIVE QUESTIONS THAT CHARACTERIZE TEACHER OBSERVATION

+ **Purpose**—What is the purpose of this observation? Is it to provide anecdotal and objective feedback to the teacher for purposes of self-evaluation, or is it to document teacher performance for evaluative/employment purposes?

+ **Who and What**—Who is to conduct the observation and what kinds of data are to be gathered?

+ **How**—How will these data be gathered: by instrumentation, script taping, videotaping, audio taping?

+ **Who**—Who will analyze these data to determine implications for teaching?

+ **Who**—Who will use the analyses to make value statements about the quality of teacher performance?

CONSIDERING THE ANSWERS

The answers to these questions define the scope and thrust of the school's professional growth program. Most important, they determine the degree of teacher ownership within the program. If, for example, the answer to the second, fourth, and fifth questions is "the immediate supervisor" or "an administrator," the observation is *administratively-directed*. If the answer is "a colleague group," the observation is *peer-directed*. And if the answer is "the individual teacher," the program is *self-directed*.

As evidenced in much of the literature, a combination of these three kinds of observation is desirable. A legion of writers within the past several years have indicated that linkages among the summative and formative components of the professional growth process are essential to teacher growth. To assure a complementary relationship among them, therefore, schools seeking collegial interaction have sustained a focus on these basic questions and have used them as standards to measure teacher autonomy in the professional growth process.

DISTINGUISHING BETWEEN EVALUATION
AND SUPERVISION

A further distinction will help. The supervisory programs in this book invariably consider the difference between "observation as evaluation" and "observation as supervision." Each time an observation is conducted, these programs first determine what is the focus of the process. For example, "observation as evaluation" emphasizes *valuation,* or *what is.* It is merely descriptive and looks only at the current situation, with little emphasis on enhancing strengths or remedying weaknesses. It is legitimately an administrative responsibility and reflects the school's annual task to provide a descriptive assessment of program and personnel.

Myth Number Eight: "Well-conceived programs that provide frequent evaluation of teachers by members of the hierarchy are the best process for promoting continued professional growth."

No matter how well-conceived the programs and how sensitive the members of the hierarchy, schools that focus on administrative evaluation to the exclusion of teacher self-evaluation fail to promote the kind of teacher growth that is evident in the program profiled in this chapter. "Observation as supervision" emphasizes *vision,* or *what can be.* It looks to the future. As such, it is a primary element in any process of professional growth.

"Observation as supervision" is also developmental. Its emphasis on the future requires an assessment of the current situation but only as a starting point for the continuing improvement of performance. It is ongoing and fosters the kind of feedback that is necessary for growth. It is the essential complement to "observation as evaluation" in that it extends the school's responsibility for teacher assessment beyond the mere description of performance to the *improvement* of performance.

A GOLF ANALOGY

Consider golf. Some golfers spray their shots into every hazard on the course without any knowledge of what they are doing wrong. At such times, they are desperate for help, for any answer to the question, "What am I doing wrong?" Many teachers seek answers to the same question. "Observation as evaluation" provides these answers. In fact, the best time to provide evaluation to someone is when he or she asks for it. This is true in any situation.

Other golfers are familiar with their own mistakes and actually resent frequent evaluation. They simply want their golf partners to watch them to see if the back swing is too fast or the follow-through too short. All they require is objective, observational feedback to make sure they are doing what they had planned to do. Teachers need this kind of feedback much more often than they need value judgments. The programs at the end of this chapter accommodate such a need.

The growth of peer coaching and collegial relationships between supervisors and teachers are important examples of "observation as supervision." Supervisors who work with teachers are gaining credibility as professionals because they find themselves less often giving answers and more often asking the right questions. As a result, teachers are giving them more power. That these teachers are giving supervisors permission to work with them is testimony to the validity of the programs and to the growing skills of supervisors.

THE NEED FOR A SHIFT OF FOCUS

Just how are these supervisors working differently with teachers? Well, first of all, they recognize that it can be as threatening to evaluate as it is to be evaluated. Effective evaluation requires expert power, not positional or hierarchical authority. For this reason, many supervisors become as uncomfortable as the teachers they observe. The least skilled find sanction in the roles they occupy, not the knowledge they possess or seek. The most skilled realize that evaluating a teacher, especially if he or she has been teaching conscientiously for several years, generally involves one of two basic assumptions.

The first assumption is the most obvious. Schools have assumed for years that administrators have sufficient knowledge of the teaching/learning process to make value judgments of classroom performance and to influence the professional growth as well as the employment status of teachers. Given the experience and the technical competence required of most administrators and supervisors, the assumption seems generally reliable. That they understand the complexities of teaching is consistent with the assumption. That they understand them better than all teachers, or even most teachers, is where the assumption begins to break down.

Some administrators and supervisors are the most knowledgeable people in the building regarding teaching. Most are not. If we accept that fact—and it flies in the face of a lot of tradition—then what fundamental purpose do they serve? In essence, what function can they perform to assist with the professional growth of their teaching colleagues?

That's where the second assumption comes in. Many supervisors understand the teaching/learning process but reject the "I-know-more-than-you" notion. They accept the assumption that their effectiveness is enhanced when they avoid making value judgments and when they control the process by which such value judgments are made—by the teacher.

Value judgments regarding teacher performance are decisions. Daniel Griffiths suggested a long time ago that administrators/supervisors restrict their decisions to the decision-making process and make fewer of the actual decisions. The key for effective supervision, therefore, is to make few value judgments about teaching (decisions) but to control the process by which they are made.

As evidenced in all the sample programs that follow, the easiest way to do this is to remove the decisional burden of responsibility from the supervisor and leave it with the teacher. This is where it belongs anyway. Both the teacher and the supervisor will be happier. Most important, teacher self-evaluation results in ownership of performance. To reconsider Woodrow Wilson's observation, then, supervisors should promote the illumination that comes from teacher self-assessment and avoid the heat that comes from traditional evaluation.

THE PROCESS IS SIMPLE

Every worthwhile classroom observation involves the collection of data, the kind that documents one or more areas of teacher performance. Teachers must be the first to analyze these data and, ultimately, to make preliminary decisions regarding what the data say about the quality of teaching. The process, therefore, consists of four steps:

♦ The first requires the supervisor to interpret and analyze the data regarding its implications for teaching, but to avoid sharing any conclusions with the teacher. Nothing should interfere with the teacher's self-assessment.

♦ The second step involves giving the data to the teacher. This should be done at least 24 hours before a postobservation conference. The teacher is asked to review the materials and to be prepared to discuss them when he or she meets with the supervisor.

♦ The third step involves the meeting, a time when the supervisor seeks to elicit analyses from the teacher, discuss the teacher's reactions, and help identify implications for future teaching. This "helpmate" step is not much different from those described so exhaustively in the literature.

♦ The final step involves the supervisor's written record of the teacher's self-evaluation. If written thoughtfully by the supervisor, it should contain no value judgments, but should reflect a control of the process by which such value judgments are made by the teacher. Such a process requires of the supervisor a knowledge of teaching as well as the ability to elicit appropriate responses from the teacher.

A QUICK EXAMPLE

Following is an example from a student in one of our classes, a department chair in a local high school. She submitted it to the class for critique before giving it to the teacher in her department:

> I enjoyed the way you engaged your class in the comparison of "Dulce et Decorum Est" with the final chapter of Crane's *Red Badge of Courage*. The students, particularly Tom in the front row, entered into the conversation with real enthusiasm, especially when you probed his comment that there is nothing glorious about fighting and dying for one's country.
>
> I noticed two students in the back of the class—Jim and Fred—who never paid much attention to any of the discussion. It might be wise to call on them periodically or to use Silver's "Think book" concept to get them engaged. . . .

Our class liked the tenor of the report and felt that it reflected a good relationship between the supervisor and the teacher. The critique, however, resulted in a different report, which the department chair subsequently gave to the teacher, after meeting with her to discuss the data and to encourage the teacher's self-analysis.

> You were mighty proud of that lesson! After a quick look at my script tape, you decided that your decision to compare and contrast "Dulce et Decorum Est" with the final chapter of Crane's *Red Badge of Courage* was a good strategy. You were especially pleased with—as you put it—the higher order thought process it provoked in the class, especially Tom, "who got right to the heart of the lesson with his comments."
>
> You were somewhat disturbed about Jim and Fred and their apparent reluctance to "dive in." You observed that they do this quite often. After some discussion, you decided to formulate a few questions—"just for them"—the kind that are likely to get a reaction from both of

them. I'd like to watch the strategy at some time in the future; I want to try it in my class with a couple of people who always seem to have their minds somewhere else. . . !

After giving the revised observation report to the teacher, the supervisor indicated that she felt better about the whole process because she didn't have to make any value judgments. The teacher made all of them, and the supervisor merely "recorded" them. She was pleased that her skills involved helping the teacher analyze the data, not fending off attacks from a frustrated teacher who disagreed with her judgment of the class. She enjoyed the task of being a "helpmate" throughout the process.

The teacher liked it, too. Because the supervisor makes no value judgments/decisions, the supervisor's involvement in the process is more acceptable to the teacher. The process, therefore, is less threatening to both of them and more supportive of their respective positions in the school, the teacher as professional and the supervisor as a knowledgeable colleague. Most important, the teacher is more likely to accept the substance of the report, to work harder to improve areas of weakness, and to seek the supervisor's help when needed.

THEORY-BASED PRACTICE

Such programs of collaborative supervision are consistent with accepted theory. Daniel Griffiths, a prominent theorist in educational administration for the past several decades, indicated years ago that the person who oversees the decisional process and makes the fewest terminal decisions is the best liked and the most powerful person in the organization. Such a person provides the framework within which decisions are made by others in the organization.

When teachers have the opportunity to share their expertise regarding curriculum and other key elements in the school program, they gain an increased sense of autonomy and self-esteem. These feelings are enhanced even more when teachers make the decisions/value judgments that provide the direction for their own professional growth. As important for the supervisor, teachers tend to appreciate and grant power to supervisors/administrators who promote self-evaluation in others.

Rudolph Dreikurs once said, "Until I can risk appearing imperfect in your eyes, without fear that it will cost me something, I can't really learn from you." Although Dreikurs was referring to the parent/child relationship, his concept is easily as appropriate for supervisors and teachers. Trust builds the foundation, and the willingness to promote teacher self-evaluation provides the building blocks for strengthened supervisory relationships.

Because teachers appreciate and ultimately give power to such supervisors, the process is as desirable for them as it is for teachers. Supervisors feel a heavy burden of responsibility when they are expected to "have all the right answers." Their burdens are virtually eliminated when they are expected only to "ask all the right questions" and to work *with* teachers rather than *over* them.

THESE PROGRAMS ARE NOT FOR EVERYONE

Obviously, not every teacher is capable of the kind of self-evaluation that leads to ownership of performance. Those who are either inexperienced or incapable require direct assistance from supervisors. Such assistance must involve specific value judgments. Such judgments should be followed by directed experiences for the teacher that remediate areas of weakness. Knowledgeable writers in the field, however, assert that teachers requiring such assistance constitute only 5 to 10% of the typical school staff. The majority of teachers, therefore, will benefit from a process that engages them in self-evaluative activities most of the time.

The supervisors involved in the program outlined at the end of this chapter realize similar benefits. The incorporation of teacher self-assessments into observation reports promotes a willingness in teachers to engage in follow-up professional growth activities and to regard supervisors as helpmates in the process. And when supervisors are perceived as helpmates, they become immediately more effective, and their levels of self-satisfaction necessarily increase. The process is beneficial to everyone, particularly to students, who realize the greatest benefits from the professional growth experiences of their teachers.

INTEGRATING IN-SERVICE TRAINING ACTIVITIES

Myth Number Nine: "Professional growth programs in many of the nation's schools, consisting traditionally of in-service training, supervision, and evaluation, reflect the responsibility of school hierarchies to provide carefully coordinated growth experiences for their teachers."

It simply isn't happening in most schools. Several, however, have integrated in-service with supervision and evaluation as discussed in this chapter. One very successful example is discussed at the end of this chapter. This particular program looks at in-service training, supervision, and evaluation as complementary concepts, and it creates linkages among them so that they are mutually reinforcing.

For the moment, consider the images of BOOKS, MIRRORS, and RED PENCILS as "Helping Hands" that promote professional growth for teachers. Obviously, a helping hand can come to us in different ways:

♦ It may come in the form of information, the kind of well-structured, interestingly presented information that both induces and fosters our growth. Such information can provide the foundation for new or refined ways of behaving or performing tasks. For the purposes of this chapter, consider such information—a BOOK.

♦ It may come in the form of anecdotal or objective feedback regarding the specifics of a task. Such feedback can be self-perceived or provided by someone else. Usually practice is involved, often using the information that was provided earlier. Let's consider such feedback—a MIRROR.

♦   Finally, it may come in the form of advice, suggestions, or encouragement, even directives that "push" people in a certain direction. Often, such advice involves the emphasis of external criteria and/or the perceived inability of someone to meet those criteria. Let's consider this helping hand—a RED PENCIL.

Well-integrated professional growth programs use all three images in complementary ways. Information (*In-service training*) is provided; practice and feedback (*Supervision*) are encouraged; and quality control (*Evaluation*) is used to determine the need for more information and/or practice. The process, therefore, is cyclical, involving teachers in ongoing growth and renewal, using each element of the professional growth process to complement the other two.

In such programs, in-service training is not the neglected child in the family of professional growth activities. It shares equal treatment with evaluation, the traditional "favored child" of the family, and new arrivals like peer coaching and self-directed supervision. In other schools, in-service training continues to involve "one-shot deals" that feature knowledgeable and, most important, entertaining speakers who share their insights with teachers to inspire them.

We met once with a secondary school principal who indicated that his purpose in providing in-service programming was to stimulate his staff, to "excite" them. He even went so far as to say that traditional in-service programs were boring and that he wanted his staff to have "fun." So he developed an in-service format that featured "Dressing for Success," "The Basics of CPR," even videos of his most recent fishing trip. We agreed with the need for enjoyment but asked one question: "Are you saying that learning can't be fun?"

Obviously, "excitement" itself is not the answer. In fact, excitement without appropriate follow-up often leads only to frustration. Examples of this are far too numerous, even too obvious to mention! The point is, teachers need follow-up activities in order to integrate in-service information. And such information should relate to professional competencies, not to the principal's fishing trip. Several schools across the country realize this. They understand the relationship that exists among the supervisory and evaluative processes in the building and its in-service activities, especially as all three constitute the heart of the professional growth program.

WHEN COLLEGIALITY DOESN'T WORK

Some programs have been successful; others have not. Those of us who labor daily in the field have watched scores of unsuccessful schools struggle for long hours to make something grow. And they all seem to make the same mistakes. The characteristics that the unsuccessful schools have in common and the insights they involve are important for each of us to recognize before seeking to implement such programs.

The first characteristic involves the heart and soul of collegiality, yet it seems to be the least observed by schools interested in promoting the concept. It is also the most ironic. Many schools develop whole processes of collegial supervision without engaging the teaching staff in collegial planning. They create programs to promote collaborative planning, but such programs are planned and implemented unilaterally. To make matters worse, they are then imposed on the staff as solutions to undefined problems. It's no wonder that teachers are often left wondering what this collegiality thing is all about.

At this point, only the creative energy that surrounds new ideas can sustain them through the first year of operation. During this first year, teachers function within the programs, questioning their value but discovering the often unplanned but inevitable benefits that result from increased interaction. Even the benefits of this interaction, however, ultimately give way to the staff's inability to understand and use the skills required of collegial supervision.

This suggests the second reason why such programs fail. The ability of participants to observe each other and, later, to discuss their observations in nonthreatening and objective ways is directly proportional to the ultimate success of the program. Teachers who are unable to focus on important teaching behaviors, thorough data-gathering procedures, and relevant and nonthreatening questions before and after the observation are likely to find the experience frustrating and profitless.

Schools interested in implementing such programs, therefore, must involve teachers in the initial planning activities by conducting needs assessments, being sensitive to the problems that confront teachers in the classroom, and listening to their suggested solutions. The teachers next must learn how to help each other throughout the process.

They must learn how to gather objective, anecdotal data during classroom observations, the kind that recreate the lesson and provide a mirror for the teacher to promote reflection. They must learn how to meet before the observation to determine what data are to be gathered and how they are to be gathered. Finally, they must learn to share the data and discuss them with each other in nonevaluative ways so that teachers can apply what they have learned to subsequent classroom experiences.

Most importantly, schools must be sure to link collegial activities in supervision with in-service training themes and subsequent teacher evaluation procedures. Many teachers are unable to reconcile the data and comments made by colleagues with the subsequent evaluative comments made by administrators. Sometimes the two have little in common. And, in many schools, rarely do in-service programs relate functionally with subsequent supervisory and/or evaluative activities.

So what do we do? Let's look at a couple programs for some answers.

PROGRAM NUMBER ONE

We knew a principal, now retired, who gathered his staff at the end of the school year to recap the year and to discuss needs for the next year. He then asked the teachers to identify topics that required their collective attention, such topics as working with the unmotivated student, question and answer technique in the classroom, and cooperative learning.

He even threw in some of his own ideas: multicultural sensitivity, technology in the classroom, reflective techniques for teachers, and other topics that were evident in the literature or that emerged from his detailed review of the accumulation of teacher observations conducted that year. By reviewing all the observations, he invariably found a few that recurred among several different teachers. Because the teachers remembered them during the end-of-the-year meeting, they were willing to consider them for in-service themes for the next school year.

He next asked the staff to select an area that was of particular interest to them and to identify "experts" they knew who might lead in-service training sessions in that area. Once the staff has selected a topic, they were assigned to a group with others who had selected the same topic. He then identified consultants to meet with each small group a minimum of three times a year. Between each of these meetings, a period usually lasting 2 months, the group members were asked to tandem or team with each other to "practice what the consultant preached."

One or two additional in-service programs were provided during the year to help them engage meaningfully in such "practice." Such programs provide a focus on observing and conferencing skills. The combination of small-group in-service and the collegial supervision they engaged in between meetings led ultimately to the administrative evaluation of their future use of the concepts in the classroom. With such evaluation, the professional growth cycle for this school was complete. The teachers had experienced in-service, supervision, and evaluation activities, all united by a common theme.

As important as anything else in the process, the teachers had been involved collaboratively in the planning of the activities. They also

+ Selected the in-service themes;
+ Had a hand in identifying the consultants;
+ Had been involved with colleagues to practice what they have learned; and
+ Had accepted the future reality of administrative evaluation to see if the concepts had been integrated into their instructional repertoires.

Schools interested in implementing such programs without involving teachers from start to finish in such planning run the risk of failure or, more likely, of only marginal success. Collaborative programs must be planned and operated collaboratively, and they must acknowledge the needs of teachers to learn how to engage in collegial activities. Data-gathering techniques and conferencing skills must be learned.

Graduate-level courses abound for administrators to learn such skills; teachers require the same quality of instruction. And both need the opportunity to practice them. The need to be objective, anecdotal, and nonevaluative runs counter to the traditional predispositions of teachers and administrators. Without such skills, however, collegial programs will continue to flourish more in the literature than in actual practice.

Another program, the Deerfield High School (Deerfield, IL) Collegial Consultation program provides further illustration.

DEERFIELD HIGH SCHOOL
DEERFIELD, ILLINOIS

COLLABORATIVE COMPONENTS

- Collegial Consultation or peer coaching process has been in place over a decade and complements the larger supervision process
- Faculty volunteers their participation and are guaranteed that the work of the team is confidential
- Collegial Consultation teams merge a peer clinical supervision model and group problem-solving model for assisting each others' professional development
- Training, consultation time, and professional development credits are built into the process
- Program goal is to collaboratively develop and enhance teacher skills that will, in turn, be used successfully in the intervention process for students who are no performing
- Teachers originated and continue to operate the program; it is an example of teacher leadership and collaboration

OVERVIEW

As early as 1982, Deerfield High School, in the Chicago north shore suburb of Deerfield, with its district counterpart, Highland Park High School, developed their Collegial Consultation Program which reaches out to regular classroom teachers, as well as counselors and other support personnel, with the goal of becoming agents of change in the classroom. Their purpose is to clinically observe each other's professional work, to offer support and specific strategies for improvement, and to learn to apply diagnostic teaching skills in their classrooms.

Over the years, this peer coaching model has evolved and been sustained by participating faculty who believe it is an essential element of continuing professional growth. The original impetus for the program arose out of the frustration of teachers assigned to classes of "students with learning difficulties." From their perspective, assistance from central office and other sources was not enough. The fledgling Collegial Consultation Program emerged from their meetings to problem-solve the situation. Today, teams of four (who most likely do NOT come from the same discipline) are systematically trained during a summer workshop to observe and categorize teaching behaviors, providing anecdotal evidence to support their evaluations of the class. One of the four team members serves as team leader and facilitator. Participants then learn to share in strategy sessions. The focus is on meeting student needs and often the strategy sessions grapple with such topics as "Why is this student with auditory processing deficits having such a difficult time with this subject?"

PROGRAM HIGHLIGHTS

Deerfield and Highland Park are typical midwestern, upper middle-class high schools committed to providing the best of resources and technology to the students and faculty. The peer coaching process described, however, can be and has been developed in many schools throughout the country, regardless of the socioeconomic status of the community.

At its most basic level, groups of education colleagues from diverse content areas come together to use a peer clinical observation model/system that culminates in constructive feedback and strategies for improvement in a nonthreatening, confidential atmosphere. Over the years, however, the process has become much more. As teams are first focused on learning and improving instruction, as trust level builds and risk taking occurs, affective areas may also be explored. Perhaps the most important issue revolves around the emotional factors at work which are affecting a student's (or a teacher's) performance. Another perspective on this same issue is: how do the teacher's uncertainties about exposing his or her professional weaknesses replicate the student's uncertainties in the classroom? When this deeper level is finally probed, the opportunities for professional growth support really begin to open up.

This district program was, as explained earlier, born out of need. Twelve years ago, teachers of lower level classes cried for help in motivating and developing new learning strategies for their students. Although tracking students is under close research scrutiny in the 1990s, the response then was to explore and develop a model for sharing, which today has the formal name of the Collegial Consultation Program. The administration, it should be noted, supported the teacher efforts from the beginning.

Also over the years, professional in-services, workshops, and consultants have been engaged for the district professional development plan which incorporates suggestions from the Collegial Consultation teams. It is typical today, for example, for a collegial team to engage in eight training sessions throughout the year in which role playing are among the strategies used to respond to issues and questions that arise from team experiences.

Deerfield principal John Scornovoco accounts for the success of the program over the years: "First, it permits teachers to focus their energies and attention on growth without the anxieties and concerns that arise when a supervisor is involved. Second, the program is totally voluntary."

Currently, about 60% of the faculty are involved in the clinical observation model, a traditional model of teacher evaluation conducted by chairs, about 25% in the Collegial Consultation model, and 15% in the Self-Directed model in which the teacher identifies a goal, reports on progress, and documents progress through portfolio or other forms of assessment.

The Collegial Consultation Program has been sustained through the testimonials of its participants. District teachers often choose to rotate through the various supervision models, electing the chair observation one year, and peer coaching the next. Feedback over time also indicates that faculty trusts the process; no violations of confidence have surfaced. Finally, it has faculty ownership. A teacher coordinator, currently a Business Education teacher with one period daily release time, demonstrates a passion for the program's continued success.

THE PROCESS

In both high schools, past and current team members, plus administration members and the faculty coordinator, informally recruit participants for the coming year. Communication is deliberately aimed at new people as the staff development-peer coaching thrust of this nonjudgmental program is explained. A training workshop of 20 hours duration is held in early summer where new recruits and veteran participants learn or review the basic assumptions, philosophy, and meaning of the 7-stage process. Role playing and videotapes from previous years help participants master procedural and process steps. Participants are divided into teams of four, cross-discipline and mixed between the two high schools, Deerfield and Highland Park. There are also designated team roles that are switched throughout the year, making sure team members play all roles. There is the process observer who leads the analysis portions of the process, making sure the "big picture" is not lost. The post observation conference leader leads the strategy session and the feedback coordinator gives the one-on-one feedback at the very end of the process.

The process itself, outlined in booklet form, is described in the following phases:

- *Phase One*—The very first informal observation is done in September of the school year. Each teacher participant visits a teacher in the program for one period. This observation is a "get your feet wet" transition into the process and is not tied to the coaching/observation phases. The intent is to see what it"s like and practice "scripting" the observation with no obligation to share.

- *Phase Two*—The preobservation conference is conducted by the teacher to be observed with the other three colleagues in attendance. The teacher explains to his/her peers the goals of the lesson, what observers should be looking for, what this teacher expects to learn in the post conference. (See special forms in Appendix}

- *Phase Three*—The preobservation conference is then followed by the actual teaching period which is observed by the other three team members. Each four-member team devotes 4½ full days to the process, including 12 half-days "out of the classroom."

- *Phase Four*—This phase is called the strategy session which works on two levels. (Note: Several phases are usually completed in 1 day.) The teacher who was observed takes time alone to reflect on the teaching experience. The teacher compares the original objectives, requests for feedback, and what actually happened. In this phase, the teacher can try to anticipate the feedback. While the teacher observed is reflecting, the three peer observers meet together to share observations, review the preconference expectations, and decide how to handle the feedback session. Experience has proven that it is more effective to concentrate on only one or two items.

- *Phase Five*—The feedback session is always led by the teacher who was observed. The teacher leads with questions that the others answer and amplify during the discussion. The tone is always supportive and caring. As one teacher reported, "My observation team are like consultants who help me grow professionally. In business, you would pay big bucks for this."

- *Phase Six*—When the feedback session is concluded, the process conference is conducted with only the observers. The observers step-back and analyze "from beginning to end." Was the teacher comfortable? Did we participate or did one person dominate? How can we improve?

- *Phase Seven*—Like the September observation, phase seven is separated from the other phases which can (with planning) take place in 1 day. The closure phase is conducted within 3 to 7 days of the observation, and feedback sessions. One team member contacts the teacher who was observed in an informal setting. In a "reflection mode," the two discuss all the previous phases. Sometimes the teacher will have incorporated a suggestion from the feedback session and can report on how it worked in a subsequent class. Anything and everything about the process is discussed. All discussions are confidential. Issues of confidentiality and trust have never been violated in the long history of this program.

WHAT CAN WE LEARN?

The research on clinical supervision reinforces what we know about peer observations; both the observer and the observed can learn much about themselves and the teaching-learning process. Over time, if given support and allowed to develop naturally, Collegial Consultation can address sensitive issues of our profession. Collegial Consultation will only thrive in a climate where the process is voluntary and not tied to the summative supervision process of the district and state. Success of this process must rely on expert, not positional, authority. It fits well with districts or schools that view themselves as a community of learners, those who adopt the Senge philosophy of mastering the "five disciplines."

The role played by the principal and administration is one of providing support, resources, and recognition of its value. Concrete support, e.g., allocation of training resources, shows whether the district is sincere in viewing the potential of peer coaching. As important, however, are the symbolic actions of the leaders in charge. Are they cheerleaders for the process? Do they encourage the volunteers, make sure parents and community know and appreciate the participants' involvement? Most important, do the administrators view the program as an integral part of the system? Is peer coaching or Collegial Consultation, whatever the name, a part of the professional development program that is key to the success of your school vision?

In Deerfield-Highland Park, teachers are encouraged, but not required, to share their final evaluation papers. (Figure 5.1, which appears on page 107, is an example of an evaluation form.) From these, the district's curriculum director selects and prints a *Journal of Action Research*, not only recognizing the accomplishments of the faculty, but sharing more broadly among the other professionals. Also, at the beginning of each school year, a booklet of goals for all of the collegial team members is published, thereby supporting sharing of another sort.

Finally, those who are contemplating a model of peer coaching will want to learn from some of the Deerfield-Highland Park experience. Teachers and administrators agree that the major obstacle is the commitment of time, beginning with the teachers' reluctance (in this case) to leave the classroom the equivalent of 12 half-days during the year. It is a tribute to the success of the program that once engaged, the issue rarely surfaces again.

Also, it is important to anticipate the program evolving to meet new needs. In this district's case, "specialization teams," made up of former collegial team members who are working on individual projects, are now a second tier of the process. An example of a "specialization team" is currently working in Highland Park High School. The team involves regular education teachers and special education teachers working to coordinate their teaching efforts to assist in main streaming the students.

Peer coaching models bring professional development rewards that exceed all expectations. Success requires support from the administration, including (in most models) money for substitutes, confidentiality and commitment from participants.

SCHOOL STATISTICS

Deerfield High School
1959 Waukegan Road
Deerfield, IL 60035

Principal: John Scornovoco

Number of students: 1200
Grades: 9–12
Number of faculty: 120

FIGURE 5.1. COLLEGIAL CONSULTATION PROGRAM, DEERFIELD HIGH SCHOOL

COLLEGIAL CONSULTATION

Pre-Observation Data

Observation:

Teacher _____   Date _____ Room _____

Class   _____   Period _____ Time _____

Level _____ Year _____   Pre-Conference:

                             Date _____ Room _____

                             Campus _____ Time _____

Providing Context for Observation

1. Briefly describe concepts, activities, content that have been developed immediately prior to this observation. What are you building on?

2. List the objectives for this class session.

    At the end of this class period, the STUDENT will be able to:

- 2 -

3. List the strategies/activities you will employ to help
    students achieve these objectives.

4. How do these objectives fit into your long-range/course
    objectives?

5. How will you know that the students have achieved these
    objectives?

- 3 -

Observation Feedback

What particular teaching behaviors do you want monitored? Check
or list the items on which you particularly want feedback.

_____ Lesson Design/Structure   _____ Time Utilization

    _____ Anticipatory Set

    _____ Objectives   _____ Student Involvement

    _____ Instructional Input

        _____ Right brain   _____ Clarity

        _____ Questioning   _____ Flexibility

        _____ Thinking Skills   _____ Enthusiasm

        _____ Visual

        _____ Auditory   _____ Classroom

        _____ Tactual/Kinesthetic   Management

    _____ Modeling

    _____ Check for Understanding   _____ Other

    _____ Guided Practice   _____

    _____ Independent Practice   _____

    _____ Closure   _____

and/or

I am having a particular problem with

and need suggestions on

- 4 -

Special Considerations

Are there any special group or individual characteristics or circumstances of which the team should be aware?

Please have this data prepared and sent so that observer has material BEFORE the pre-observation conference.

POST OBSERVATION CONFERENCE FORM

The Post Observation Conference must be held within seven days of the Collegial Observation. A copy of the bottom portion of this form is to be sent to the Team Leader and to the Coordinator.

POST OBSERVATION SCHEDULE:

_____, _____, _____, _____
day   date   time   place

At the Post Observation Conference, the observed teacher should reflect on and discuss the item(s) which were of significant value to him or her, and also express any concerns he or she may have about the experience.

Date of Collegial observation_____

COPY FOR
COORDINATOR   Teacher observed_____

Date of Post observation conference_____

Team member involved_____

Comments: (if any)

Date of Collegial observation_____

TEAM
LEADER   Teacher observed_____
COPY
Date of Post observation conference_____

Team member involved_____

Comments: (if any)

REFERENCES

Costa, A. 1982. Supervision for Intelligent Teaching. *Search Model Unlimited*. Orangevale, CA.

Hunter, M. 1976. *Improved Instruction*. El Segundo, CA: TIP Publications.

Koehler, M. Inservice: Education's Neglected Child. *American Secondary Education*. Bowling Green, OH: Bowling Green State University and the Ohio Association of Secondary School Administrators.

Koehler, M. 1990. Self-Assessment in the Evaluation Process. *The NASSP Bulletin*. Reston, VA: The National Association of Secondary School Principals.

Farts of this chapter were reprinted with permission of the Helen Dwight Reid Educational Foundation from Koehler, M."Back to the Basics of Supervision." *The Clearing House*, Vol. 62, Jan. 1989, pp. 220–221, published by Heldref Publications, 1319 18th St., NW, Washington, DC 20036–1802. Also: Koehler, M. "When Collegiality Doesn't Work." *The Clearing House*. Future issue.

6

THE HIERARCHY AND PARENT INVOLVEMENT

Collaboration with the parent community is as critical today as ever in our nation's history, and perhaps more difficult. In an age of daily advances in communication technology, opportunities for ongoing dialogue and consensus-building among segments of our society seem to be declining. Linked by a comprehensive media network, we are separated by a confusion of social values and vested interests. One result is a series of startling changes in our social behavior.

In a recent 16-year period, for example, the number of children living with unwed mothers increased by 620%! The implications of such a statistic are enormous. It means that fully half of all single mothers and their children live in poverty. It means that the current statistic indicating that one in every nine youngsters will be in court by the age of 18 probably will increase within the next several years.

It suggests reasons underlying current statistics that just under a million youngsters are child prostitutes, that some 2,000 are listed as suicides each year, and that "handgun homicide" is the second leading cause of death for boys aged 15 to 19. It also explains the increase in crime on our streets and in our schools. Our schools suffer more than half a million shakedowns, robberies, and attacks every month.

Many of the children who attend these schools spend most of the day in fear and extend their cycle of poverty by dropping out of school. Twenty-five to 30% of our school-aged children drop out of school (the statistic is higher in major metropolitan areas) into a world that is unable to accommodate them. In the 1950s, more than half of the nation's school-aged youngsters dropped out of school, but they entered a labor force wherein 60% of the jobs were "blue-collar." Today, only 6 to 10% of jobs are blue-collar.

Thousands of students leave school each year with no prospects for employment and often turn to crime or welfare for survival. Their lives are complicated further by an absence of direction in the home. Approximately half of all marriages in the United States end in divorce, the highest rate in all the world's technologically advanced countries. This accounts for a recent 135% increase in children living with divorced mothers.

Obviously, most of these mothers are in the labor force, returning home each night to the uniquely challenging task of raising children with little or no support from a marriage partner. When such mothers are unmarried teenagers, they are likely to drop out of school and face the prospects of long-term poverty. Recent census figures indicate that 20% of the children in this country live in poverty.

Fortunately, many single mothers are successful in providing both the financial and the emotional support their children require, but they are paying a high price. They expend enormous amounts of emotional and psychic energy each day to maintain a job and raise a family. Even in two-parent families, maternal employment has increased by over 60%, leaving children with less parental contact during the day.

The job of the school is not to judge a parent's decision to work. Most single mothers are left with no other alternative, and many do the job with startling success. More appropriately, schools must provide the support systems such families require to raise well-adjusted children. They must also recognize that changes taking place within the family are being further affected by social and technological influences in the society.

Within the past 20 years, for example, the average consumption of books by youngsters in this country has declined by over 300%. Add to this the fact that the average high school graduate spends 12,000 hours in the classroom and 18,000 in front of the television set. Then consider that within the next 20 years high school students may experience a 100% increase in knowledge every 80 to 90 days. It becomes obvious that traditional ways of teaching and working with parents and students will have to undergo significant changes if schools are to be successful.

WHAT ARE THE RESPONSES FROM SCHOOL SYSTEMS?

Education has responded to the knowledge explosion and social pressures with cooperative learning, the voucher system, and recent technological innovations such as interactive computers. We continue to consider alternatives to current practice such as block scheduling, collegial observation, and authentic assessment to accommodate the changing needs of students. Such responses seem appropriate, especially when they move beyond trends and actually improve the learning experiences of students.

Much more, however, needs to be done, some of which involves common sense and a basic understanding of system theory. Any school system operates in a larger system and, according to system theorists, must satisfy the expectations of its environment if it is to survive. Open systems share materials and energy with their environments, exchanging inputs and outputs with them. To the extent that systems fail to promote such interaction with their environments, they compromise their own effectiveness.

Experience teaches us that some schools are less open than others. Some rarely get into their environments to exchange energy and information. They interact infrequently with the surrounding community and then only to provide an occasional PTA Night or a series of sporting events. The relative isolation that results promotes the school's attention to curriculum, instruction, and the delivery of its ancillary services but rarely in relation to the changing needs of students and parents.

The isolated analysis of the school system, therefore, without regard to the systems which are in mutual interaction with it, results in a ritualized continuation of the school's educational programs. Socially mandated changes in curriculum, methods of instruction, and the delivery of such ancillary programs as guidance and special education services are virtually impossible without a synthesis of the several systems that influence the development of youngsters, only one of which is the school.

The synthesis of these several systems is accomplished when they sustain a continuing dialogue, sharing expectations, needs, interferences, and opportunities that exist among them. Consider the recent statistic indicating that almost one in four households contains a person living alone. This statistic has almost doubled in the last 28 years, indicating, among other things, a national increase in life expectancy.

Communities across the country, therefore, enjoy growing populations of elderly citizens who, still vital and energetic, can provide a valuable resource for any school system. They represent unique historical and philosophical perspectives, a variety of fascinating life experiences, refined knowledge, and integrated value systems that are useful to teachers in any area of the curriculum.

Elderly citizens also represent needs for social contact that young people can satisfy. Several schools across the country have developed "Outreach" programs that team students and elderly adults in shared experiences, such as Christmas parties, outings to plays and the zoo, and school functions like variety shows and sporting events.

Such programs can be cocurricular as when combined with sociology or family living classes, or they can be extracurricular as when offered as student activities. Some few schools even offer classroom experiences in television production as well as extracurricular programs that provide news programs to local access cable stations. Such programs provide hands-on learning experiences for students and important information for the adult community.

Coalitions of teachers and students often work together to develop videotaped science labs and other classroom experiences that can be broadcast locally for students who are home ill. They also produce educational programs for the adult community, recognizing the value of life-long learning and the several opportunities offered by new technology.

Such schools are in the vanguard of a movement that probably will revolutionize the school's responsibilities to the adult community. Parents and other adults in the community not only deserve a voice in the determination of school policy and planning activities but increased opportunities to extend their own lives as students, benefiting from ever-expanding communication networks that can educate as well as inform.

Genetic engineers indicate that a child born today could enjoy a life expectancy of 125 years. Many of today's elementary students will live to be well over 100. Such students as adults may be required to change jobs seven or eight times during their lifetimes. Twelve years of mandated education will no longer be sufficient to provide the periodic vocational training and the ongoing exposure to a changing social environment that adults, even very elderly adults, will require.

THE COMMUNITY CONNECTION

Schools in the relatively near future, therefore, will not only accept but promote change. As the social institution primarily responsible for examining and promoting cultural values, as well as the expectation of lifelong learning in all students, schools can expect the continued evolution of their role in the community. Many of today's educators complain about the widening scope of their responsibilities, claiming topics such as driver training, sex education, and personal and social values are not the responsibility of today's school.

Current trends, however, seem to indicate that such responsibilities will widen even further within the next several years. The continued dissolution of the family unit, the impact of new technology, and the random changes in our social values seem to leave room for little else. School administrators, therefore, must promote input from parents and other adults in the community not only to meet the needs of students but to identify the emerging needs of adults.

THE PRINCIPLES OF SYNERGY REVISITED

Effective organization requires such community collaboration. Just a brief review of two relevant theories provides the reasons. Systems theory stipulates that systems require an exchange of energy and resources with their environments to be successful. The concept of synergy asserts that such an exchange promotes the mutual cooperation that results in the magnified output of the individual elements in the system.

> *Myth Number Ten:* "Education's hierarchy, recognizing the basic principles of systems theory, encourages its subsystems (generally the school's individual departments) to maintain a constant exchange of energy and resources with the parent community and other significant school populations."

In a truly open school system, this statement is true. In most school systems, however, most of which are open or closed by varying degrees, this statement is not as true. Nor is it false, because most schools provide traditional PTA Nights at school, a variety of sporting events, plays, and musical programs, and teacher-parent committees, most of which provide some degree of interaction between the school and the parent community.

Other schools, however, supplement such parent-involvement programs with consensus-building activities, needs assessments involving curriculum and the extracurricular program, the control of student behavior, potential uses of new technology, and collaborative planning groups to address other areas of mutual concern. Such schools go beyond a simple sharing of information by actively engaging parents in planning activities that involve the heart and soul of the school program and that capitalize on the synergy created when teachers and parents identify mutual needs and share ideas.

ACKNOWLEDGING AND ACCOMMODATING CHANGING NEEDS

Any social institution, whether a school, a political body, or a family, that constantly reacts to emerging needs invariably struggles to deal with them. Conversely, the social institution that proactively anticipates such needs rarely finds them to be significant problems. The difference between reactive planning and proactive planning is the difference between seeing a doctor before or after the onset of serious illness. It can mean the difference between life and death.

Proactive planning invariably involves some kind of process. Collaborative people are process oriented; they recognize that well-conceived strategies for coalescing the thinking of intelligent people often anticipate problems—before they become problems. Avoiding a problem beforehand is much easier than reacting to it afterward, particularly if it is serious and requires immediate action.

Education is facing a crossroads. It may not involve a life-and-death situation, although the problems confronting schools could so enervate them that they might lose the will to continue seeking solutions for them. Consider the significant number of metropolitan teachers working in schools that represent 30 to 40 different languages. English literature or American history teachers face insurmountable obstacles when teaching such students. In many instances they give up, and the children drop out of school to expand statistics that reflect increases in crime and poverty.

WHERE DOES SUCH PROACTIVE PLANNING START?

Logically, it starts with all educators at all levels, and it involves students, parents, and other adults in the community. Abraham Maslow has taught all of us that the higher order needs of persons are not satisfied until their lower order needs have been met. In other words, hungry or fearful children are unable to learn, no matter how creative the teaching, and students who are denied a sense of belonging—for whatever reason—are unable to gain a sense of self or to find ways to realize their potential.

Perhaps this is one reason why affirmative action programs provoked so much controversy across the country. They represented a reactive solution to a very real problem. To make matters worse, the solution was implemented after the problem had caused its greatest damage. Certain persons were selected preferentially for employment and university placement because of their minority status, in many instances regardless of their qualifications.

The early learning experiences of these minority members had failed, for whatever reason, to provide the qualifications they needed to compete with nonminority members for jobs and university placement. Obviously, the reasons for such inadequate preparation are multifold and are found somewhere in our current and past history. Solutions to inadequate preparation, however, are not found in history books. They are found in the minds of fair-thinking administrators who recognize that adequate preparation for jobs and college is a function of each student's *early learning experiences*, regardless of their minority status.

Consider an analogy. Mike, one of the authors of this book, does a lot of speaking at conventions and workshops across the country about the student-athlete situation. He is convinced, for example, that the NCAA and groups like the Knight Commission have helped assure the fair treatment of student athletes in college. He is now convinced, however, that high schools have to assure a reasonable approach to competitive athletics and an appropriate academic experience for each student.

They will accomplish this only by dialoguing among themselves and with young athletes and their parents about the realities of college athletics and the need for an appropriate education. Only then will high schools and colleges effectively combat the social circumstances that highlight athletics as a yellow brick road out of the inner city and into a world of fame and fortune.

Interestingly, these same social circumstances affect the learning experiences of all students, not just athletes. Entire communities are staggering under the weight of increased crime, relentless poverty, and the general dissolution of the family unit. Such circumstances now require elementary and secondary schools to dialogue more frequently and meaningfully with parents, not just to receive input from influential community members but to collaborate with the less influential about ways to meet their needs.

Fortunately, some schools have acknowledged such a need and are providing opportunities for students to engage with elderly citizens, for parents to discuss marriage and parenting, for coalitions of parents and teachers to explore and respond to political and economic issues in the state and local community, and for entire families to influence the scope of school decision-making regarding curriculum, student behavior, and school policy. Madison Middle School 2000 uses the World Wide Web as its "window to the world." The school itself is a city's response to a segment of the community who felt alienated and betrayed when their promised "new school" was slow in coming. Its bold venture into technology based integrated learning is the result of a university partnership. The curriculum use of themes selected by the students involves them in research and problem based learning with a potential for placing new meaning to the term "global learning."

MADISON MIDDLE SCHOOL 2000
MADISON, WISCONSIN

COLLABORATIVE COMPONENTS

- Technology based, integrated learning in core areas of math, science, and communication
- Community partnerships with university, business, and parents
- Curriculum developed from themes selected by the students of this middle school
- Student learning focused on context, mirroring what we do and how we act in the real world
- Primary partnership with computer science department of local university

OVERVIEW

When educators talk about student participation in school governance, they are usually referring to rules of behavior and decisions that relate to discipline, but certainly not the curriculum choices that are traditionally the role and responsibility of the teaching profession. If curricular involvement is rare at the high school level, it is almost nonexistent for middle level students. Madison Middle School 2000 in Madison, Wisconsin, is using the Internet as a tool to help students and teachers see their roles differently, that of a learning partnership. MMS 2000 has a culturally diverse population of both students and staff. It was established 3 years ago as an experimental school to explore new ways to teach and to learn. There are three major strands to the school, the first being a multicultural education component. The second is integrated thematic instruction. This means that all subject areas, including art and music, are centered around a theme; students help select those themes. The third major strand involves the Internet as the access to information from databases and libraries around the world. For most subject areas, the Internet is used in place of text books.

How did this school emerge as an experimental model developed by Madison School District staff in collaboration with parents, community and business leaders? The idea came out of a committee, composed of the above stake-holders, formed to design a school for the city's South side. For years, that community pleaded for a neighborhood middle school to serve the mainly minority children who live there and are bused to a variety of schools as part of district-wide desegregation plans. Everything about School 2000— from the overall approach to learning, to the racial mix of teaching staff and student body, to the size of classes—has been designed to give students of varying backgrounds the individual attention they need to succeed academically and ultimately, in an ever-changing work place.

PROGRAM HIGHLIGHTS

The total school size is 240 students, with 80 students at each grade level, sixth, seventh, and eighth. The limited enrollment provides for personalized attention for individual students as well as easy access to all of the technology tools and other resources. The size (as continuing research studies show) fosters a sense of connection to other students, teachers and parents. Accelerated progress is the expectation for every student.

Dr. Offie Hobbs, principal, holds a Ph.D. in educational administration from Kansas State University. Admittedly, the teacher selection criteria for MMS 2000 is not available to all schools, although he sees his school as a prototype for new century learning. He is not apologetic for having had the opportunity to select his teaching team, passionately believing that public school education will benefit from "pioneers like us" who can move out and explore new ways of learning and apply them to all children. Teacher selection criteria included:

- Willingness to tailor the program to meet the needs of all students
- Superior teaching skills
- An understanding of diverse cultures
- A proven record of student achievement and success

The composition of the staff reflects the ethnic and racial diversity of the student group.

Hobbs also encourages schools to invest in the accessibility of having the Internet because it brings about partnerships needed to develop as learning communities of the future. At MMS 2000 one very important partner is the Computer Science Department at the University of Wisconsin. Through the school's Technology Resource Instructor, Barbara Spitz (who at the time was a doctoral student at the university) a connection was established with Professor Larry Landweather of the Computer Science Department. Landweather helped install an ISDN line; his department helped the school faculty configure the entire network, and the Internet became a part of it. Graduate students volunteered to work with the students and were partners in the classroom when students were learning how to use the Internet. According to Spitz, "So if it was installing software or if it was working with the hardware, or if it was something they would like to do with students with hypermedia, or in using the Internet or e-mail, they would come and volunteer their time to work with students. That was very beneficial to us!"

Another partnership that was very helpful was with Siskel Systems, a company out of California that makes Internet routers to allow the students to get out to the Internet. Again, Spiz described an interesting experience students had with John Morgridge, the CEO of Siskel Systems. He was presenting at a national conference for Siskel in Chicago and during the process of his presentation (using a software *CUCM* ("See You, See Me") over the Internet) he was able to talk to students in their classroom. They had projected the students onto a big screen so the entire Chicago audience could see the students as well. While students were "preparing" for that presentation, they came upon a man from Holland (using the software program *Sesame*) and had an interesting conversation that sparked added interest in communicating with students in other countries over the Internet using *Sesame*.

Other partnerships include Apple Computers, Inc., who allowed the school to pilot a program called *Apple Search* (which in turn, facilitates users' ability to search the Internet for needed information). Another important partner has been Pioneering Partners, an organization supported by the Governors of the Great Lakes, described as a collaboration between educators, business people, and government. The goal of this partnership is to look at educational policy and think about what might be best for students as well as the business world, and how we can get support from everybody to work together on educational policy.

Madison Middle School 2000 is demonstrating the paradigm shift that occurs when technology is integrated as a tool, not as the curriculum. Parents become engaged as their children's learning partners as their children bring home the learning process. There is a laptop computer for every student which the student may take home. They can use them for everything from writing reports and designing graphics to scanning pictures from books. The laptops generate another story about MMS 2000. Who, in their right minds would give laptops to early adolescents known for their developmental differences that include all kinds of erratic behavior typical of the age? Principal Hobbs explains with pride that in 3 years, only one computer has suffered "an accident from being dropped," and none has been lost or vandalized. Shared vision, shared expectations, and shared learning responsibilities among teachers, students and their families help sustain the record.

THE PROCESS

Madison Middle School 2000 represents a true, collaborative learning partnership between teachers and students, at an age level where many would argue that "only the adults" should be in charge. When the faculty and principal Hobbs first began planning, they intellectually embraced the philosophy of student as worker and teacher as coach-facilitator as opposed to deliverer of instruction. In the beginning stages of their planning, they further recognized that they would be pioneering in new curricular areas; they would be literally creating and developing a curriculum which they determined must evolve from the learner's natural curiosity. Hence the decision to allow students to select their own learning themes. At the beginning of the first year, in an assembly, students voted their first topic as sports, followed by animals, and health.

Unlike other conventional middle schools where state regulations and district curriculum guidelines determine what students study, MMS 2000 teachers took the students' themes and planned multimedia activities that would teach the fundamental academic skills. There are no textbooks (with the exception of math texts that were added in the Fall of 1994) because the curriculum is original, developed as students decide what they want to learn about.

Using the Internet allows students to have the real-life experience, the authentic experience of using real databases around the world, up-to-date resources for doing research and investigation of a topic. When students recently worked on a health and family unit, they used the Internet to connect to the World Health Organization, the National Institutes of Health, the White House, and to speeches President Clinton has given regarding health issues. They were able to access a wide range of resources; for example, there is a cancer database as well as an AIDS database that students were able to access. The way the school network is set up, there are CD-Roms on the network as well as the Internet. There is a section called Library Services where students have resources that they may use, electronic resources that they may use in their research like *A Guide to Periodic Literature* where they may get current magazine articles about the topic they're working on.

The Internet extends collaboration and communication for these Madison students. Each student and each faculty member has his/her own e-mail. In the most recent school year, students developed their own "home page" on the Internet which literally links them to the world. One teacher who visited Hungary last summer is working on a connect for students in Hungary. A student is exploring Key Pals Wanted on Internet, where teachers can talk to one another and request key pals from around the world. The Spanish and French teachers are hoping to connect the Madison students with their counterparts in Spanish- and French-speaking countries.

What are the challenges of this new learning process? The professional development time needed to launch and sustain this new learning model is significant in both hours and commitment. There is a constant stream of training for this school's own faculty, plus training for teachers from the university, teachers who are in preservice programs, teachers in the school district on technology. The MMS 2000 pioneers believe that the technology choice is not whether, but when. As Offie Hobbs says, "Until others are willing to try it, we're going to be in a holding pattern because it takes teachers and the administrators to get it done, to learn how to use it and say, it's not as bad as you think, let's take the kids' approach and let's be willing to explore the possibilities." The biggest challenge, then, is changing the paradigms, or mental models that most of us have regarding the use of technology as a central tool for learning.

What Can We Learn?

There are a number of questions, many of them steeped in controversy, inherent in the Madison Middle School 2000 experiment. The first has to do with "privileges and perks."

Does this charter school, which is among the first in the state of Wisconsin, take away resources, the "best teachers," selected students, for an experiment that will succeed because of additional support, not the merit of the idea? The MMS 2000 participants, including Hobbs, faculty, students, parents, and community partners, argue that they should be viewed as leaders and pioneers of what needs to happen in next century learning. These teachers have moved from deliverers of content to resource people. Students now have an ability to go out and search the Internet for information, rich in context for their individual and group learning. Students have moved from the first step of "how do I do this on my own," to engaging teachers at the third or fourth step of analysis, interpretation, and problem-solving. Teachers like the idea of saying to students, we're all learners, we're here to learn with you. And students like the idea that they're learning with adults, including the parent community.

There is also the issue of technological equity. Hobbs and staff believe that using the Internet is one of the best equalizers of information available. It works well with student achievement, it can teach students how to use the Internet, and the appropriate skills for a computer search, and Internet hunts. It does not replace the teacher! The role of the teacher becomes more significant as well as more complex as we move from teaching information to helping students synthesize, analyze and interpret their investigations. It requires teacher retraining, but considering that the knowledge explosion of global information doubles every 2 years, this is considered by many educators to be a small price to pay. Also, the assertion that any academic degree is now considered to have a "shelf-life" of less than 5 years, may mean we are doing the education profession a huge favor.

Finally, the MMS 2000 experiment forces us to take a look at what research is telling us about learning environments. Until recently, no one, certainly not large urban areas, paid much attention to the research on small schools that says students learn better and faster in smaller environments where they are known, cared about, and can receive personalized attention.

MMS 2000 staffing differs from most other Madison schools in its staffing ratio which is 20:1 versus 29:1. We also have ample evidence through the work of Sizer, Glaser, Gardner, and others, that students of all ages need more connections and exposure to "real world" experiences. It is acknowledged that school problems, e.g., continuing segregation, mirrors society's problems, e.g., segregated housing patterns. Technology, if made available to all children, can play a key role in equalizing access to information. Many eyes are on MMS 2000, but the students and teachers there are too busy building and improving their learning partnership to pay much notice. Having mastered the art and science of developing curriculum from themes suggested by the students, they are currently embarked on developing relevant authentic assessments as evidence of the students' learning. They are busy in their professional development, trying to keep on the cutting edge of developing technology with the help of their business partners. They are challenged to be faster, better, learning partners with their students. They invite the reader to watch and learn from their pioneering efforts, including the risks and the mistakes, to prove that technology is a powerful learning tool.

SCHOOL STATISTICS

Madison Middle School 2000
Temporary location (until new school is built)
Hoyt School
3802 Regent Street
Madison, Wisconsin

Grades: 6–8
Number of students: 240

Principal: Offie Hobbs
Phone: 608/833–9558

7

THE SCHOOL HIERARCHY AND THE STUDENT BODY

Scientists find clues to civilization in cultural artifacts. Consider our civilization. What cave drawings were to early paleontologists, the footage in the caverns of network television's storage rooms will be for future generations of scientists. Are there better vehicles than the soap opera and the talk show to chronicle the social evolution of contemporary America? Perhaps, but it wouldn't provide a better introduction to this chapter.

Schools have been struggling for years to satisfy society's challenge to reaffirm family and personal values. This particular challenge is only the latest in a history of expectations that have been suggested of schools from Colonial days to the present time. And, perhaps, that's as it should be. Teachers have been *in loco parentis* for many years, substituting during the greater part of each day for parents and assuming the task of teaching youngsters not only academic, but personal and social behaviors.

Always an enormous task, the job has become more complicated with each passing year. Soap operas and talk shows are just a few of the media influences that seem to be redefining normalcy in our society. Magazines, music videos, movies, and television highlight aberrant behavior to the point where adults as well as youngsters sometimes confuse it with behaviors that, in the past, were considered more acceptable.

A result is that many children and young adults have lost the anchor that formerly stabilized them in the sea of changing values that has become American society. To further complicate matters, many teachers reject society's expectation that schools provide the values training that so many youngsters desperately need. They claim that schools are unable to be all things to all people and that values are something that should be taught in the home.

Unfortunately, many homes are causing the values vacuum that plagues many students. Since 1970, the rate of unmarried parents who are cohabiting has increased six-fold. In 1970, one in 10 families was headed by a single parent. The number has increased to three in 10 today. The United States experiences more teenage illegitimate pregnancies than any other industrialized nation. In the early 1990s, the figure among whites rose to 22%, 11 times greater than the 2% in 1960. Among blacks, the figure is 68%.

In the early 1990s, one in 10 teenage girls got pregnant, half of them keeping the children. In 1970, only 5% of the 15-year-old girls in the United States had engaged in sexual intercourse. By 1988, that number had risen to 25%. Obviously, much of this accounts for the dramatic rise in single-parent households in America. To say, therefore, that many of these households lack a framework of sustaining values is not unrealistic.

It is unrealistic—and unfair—to paint all single-parent households with the same broad stroke. Many parents in this country are meeting the significant challenge of raising children without a partner. They work each day and maintain a household at night, devoting themselves to the stability and security of their children. Such parents are to be commended and cannot be confused statistically with unmarried teenage mothers who remain on welfare for 10 or more years and fail to bring a core of experience and understanding to the task of raising their children.

The children of such parents tend to engage in criminal acts and require value orientation almost from the first time they walk through the doors of a school. The school is the logical and most appropriate place to provide these values; and teachers, coaches, counselors, administrators, and even custodians are the logical people to promote them. The question is, are the nation's schools prepared to provide the framework of well-integrated and appropriately modeled values that many of today's youngsters require?

VALUES EDUCATION AND RELIGION

It is a classic understatement to say that education has been hit hard by litigious reactions to God in the school. That they shy from anything moralistic or value-laden is understandable. Perhaps they must be reminded that American pluralism is a constant cause of conflicting social and personal opinion. The fact that religious beliefs are at the core of that pluralism must not be allowed to obscure the importance of values in the school.

By their own admission, religions involve "mysteries," those unsubstantiated tenets that constitute much of the core of belief. As essential as they may be to religious doctrine, such "mysteries" can provoke among others misunderstandings, conflicting opinions, and occasional conflicts. Fortunately, however, there is nothing mysterious about basic values.

Schools need not fear litigation for emphasizing simple consideration. The current interpretation of social pluralism in our courts reflects a confusion in our society that tries to resolve all conflict with compromise. Because current interpretations of the Constitution seek a rigid separation of church and state, we prohibit religion in the schools and compromise the need to teach values. Because school hierarchies generally fear any kind of litigation, they tend to avoid controversial issues, one being values education.

An earlier chapter discussed basic systems concepts, the need for systems, for example, to operate in steady states. The school "system" promotes the status quo by assuring the institution's need to survive; it necessarily compromises external pressures for change. Because many schools see potential conflict in values education, they compromise their need to provide it. Unfortunately, compromise is like an old car. It's beat-up, slow, and uncomfortable, but it steers in the right direction—until it breaks down completely and leaves us searching for alternative destinations.

As a nation, we often find ourselves searching for alternative destinations. Past compromises, for example, have resulted in the acceptance of prayer in Congress but not in our schools; it has promoted an awareness of God on our coins but not in our classrooms. Admittedly, religion often involves compromise, but we need not compromise on the values we seek to emphasize in our nation's schools.

The values found at the core of American political and social philosophy are not mysterious. We can all agree on a core of uncompromised values that are spiritual in effect if not in name—basic consideration, honesty, fairness, reverence for life, mutual cooperation, hard work—that can become the framework for our relationships with students. Fortunately, many schools are doing just this.

Many schools, for example, are teaching dialogue in the classroom. They are teaching students to build upon each other's shared ideas, to accept new ideas nonjudgmentally, and to experience the joy of exploration, reflection, and the discovery of shared knowledge and thought. Peter Senge distinguishes "dialogue" from "discussion," which he sees as the analysis of ideas involving conflicting opinion, a process that involves the attack and defense of ideas and the ultimate selection of a "best" solution. Such a distinction suggests another of education's myths:

> *Myth Number Eleven:* "Being the primary clients of the school's program, students regularly receive opportunities from most school hierarchies to maintain or change curriculum and instruction."

This statement may be true in some schools because many of them provide processes for varying degrees of student involvement in the analysis of curriculum and instruction. Such involvement, however, is generally limited to evaluation of classroom instruction; rarely, are students engaged in the actual development of curriculum. The question asked earlier remains: Who are the primary clients of the school?

Because school hierarchies are concerned with the maintenance and survival needs of the system and, as indicated in a previous chapter, at times reflect the needs of the invisible organization, it is reasonable to assume that students are sometimes not the primary clients of the school. That many administrators regard parents and other influential members of the community the primary clients of the school has been emphasized in an earlier chapter.

Students, therefore, may not receive the breadth of involvement in curriculum development that they deserve or that seems warranted by their daily exposure to the content and processes of their learning experiences. Similarly, they may benefit both themselves and the school if given routine opportunities to influence the quality and nature of classroom instruction. Schools that routinely use the input of students receive insights they might not otherwise discover about their instructional and ancillary programs.

That education's hierarchy develops processes that promote dialogue with students not only in the classroom but throughout the school is essential if students are to experience the "value" of sharing ideas with each other and of building upon the collective thought of teachers and administrators. The experience of influencing the direction of curriculum and classroom instruction not only promotes an understanding and facility with "dialogue," it emphasizes the values of consideration, mutual cooperation, and hard work.

"Dialogue" enables teachers, administrators, and students to model the values that are important to all of us in situations that enable everyone to win. "Discussion," because it involves the attack and defense of conflicting opinion, promotes a "win-lose" situation. Certainly, it involves skills that are needed in our society, but it also promotes competition over cooperation and emphasizes student and teacher behaviors that, at times, are inconsistent with the values mentioned earlier.

Students, therefore, do not require decisional authorities when given opportunities to influence curriculum and instruction. That they engage in discussion with school personnel is less important than the dialogue they experience as they work with administrators and teachers to improve the quality of the school's learning experiences. Interestingly enough, the mere act of seeking to improve curriculum and instruction provides one of their most rewarding learning experiences.

WHAT ARE THESE VALUES?

Exactly what are the values we seek in our schools? They may vary from school-to-school, but probably will contain a common core of behaviors that are important to teachers, administrators, and parents in any community. That each of these constituencies has a hand in their development and implementation is critical if the values are to reflect the expectations of each community and to influence the behaviors of students.

"Shared" values result in shared responsibilities and a mutual willingness to promote and model them. Like teachers who accept ownership of school policies and programs they help develop, parents and students tend to "own" the values they identify as important in the school and community. The key, then, is to dialogue with students and parents and find consensus regarding the values the school will emphasize with students and teachers.

Figure 7.1 provides a starting point for promoting the dialogue within the school and community that will result in such consensus. When finally integrated into faculty and student handbooks, such a statement of values tends to serve as the school's standard of behavior and provides the framework for both teacher and student behavior in the school.

THE REALITIES OF STUDENT DISCIPLINE

This leads to a discussion of student discipline and another of the myths proposed in this book:

Myth Number Twelve: "The hierarchy provides the policies and procedures that represent the primary authority for the control of student behavior."

FIGURE 7.1. ACHIEVING A CONSENSUS OF VALUES

Following is a list of values that our school embraces. Please read the list, identify those which are most important to you, and rank them in descending order of importance, 1 being the most valued, 21 the least. Our school will determine a consensus of opinion and work closely with you and other community members to develop a program which responds to the values that we consider to be important for our students.

WE MUST HELP OUR STUDENTS:

_____ Develop social skills.

_____ Value the processes of education.

_____ Analyze experience and relationships which have brought them the greatest happiness.

_____ Identify ways to relate to society's institutions.

_____ Explore experiences that lead to lifestyle and vocational choices.

_____ Explore their personal strengths and weaknesses.

_____ Understand the increasing interdependence among segments of society.

_____ Experience and study democratic principles in action.

_____ Develop a positive self-concept.

_____ Explore people, relationships, interests, goals, et al., in relation to the basic values of our students.

_____ Discuss the what and why of their responsibilities to other people.

_____ Explore and understand the difference between needs and wants.

_____ Learn positive ways to assert their influence on society.

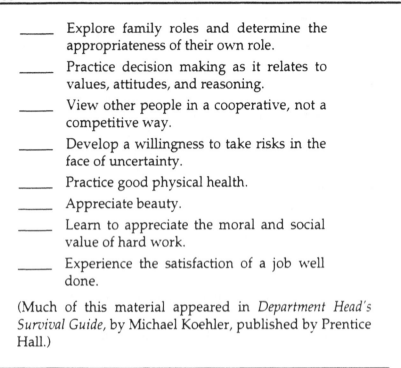

_____ Explore family roles and determine the appropriateness of their own role.

_____ Practice decision making as it relates to values, attitudes, and reasoning.

_____ View other people in a cooperative, not a competitive way.

_____ Develop a willingness to take risks in the face of uncertainty.

_____ Practice good physical health.

_____ Appreciate beauty.

_____ Learn to appreciate the moral and social value of hard work.

_____ Experience the satisfaction of a job well done.

(Much of this material appeared in *Department Head's Survival Guide,* by Michael Koehler, published by Prentice Hall.)

Such a myth is consistent with the belief that the hierarchy controls people by establishing the policies that govern what should be the purely rational characteristics of the school organization. As indicated in an earlier chapter, there is nothing "purely rational" about organizational behavior.

Nor does the hierarchy control student behavior simply by developing and expecting compliance with preestablished rules and regulations. Policies and procedures may provide a sense of direction for the school, but they must depend ultimately on the competencies of teachers and the influence of parents to promote student self-discipline and the execution of reasonable consequences for misbehavior.

Policies are predetermined decisions. They are designed to anticipate questions or problems and to promote consistency when decisions are required regarding student and teacher behavior. Because they are decisions, they reflect the values of those who make them and, if effective, the reasonable expectations of those affected by them. Policy statements, therefore, represent and reflect the body of values that guides the thinking and behavior of decision-makers.

If this set of values is mutually developed by administrators, parents, teachers, and students, the policies that bring it to life are acceptable to the people affected by them. It is essential, therefore, not only to communicate policy statements to every student in the school but to encourage them to help shape such statements. Such dialogue promotes valuable consensus in the building and makes rules governing student behavior much more acceptable to the entire student body.

Taking a Look at External and Internal Discipline

Students who help shape school policy are motivated to abide by such policy. The mere act of being involved in policy formulation is motivating to most students. Certainly, every student in the school will not engage in the actual deliberations. This will be restricted to a select group of students working in concert with administrators, parents, and teachers. But if the student body makes input and is informed routinely of progress, they will sense some ownership of anything that results from the group's study.

For our purposes, the key principle to keep in mind is that enforcement of rules and regulations is the school's response when student self-discipline breaks down. Successful school hierarchies realize that effective school discipline inheres in the willingness of students to behave in ways which are consistent with a commonly accepted and well-modeled set of values. To the extent that they have a hand in the development of such values, school discipline is even that much better.

The Hierarchy and Student Behavior: The Big Picture

Policy statements regarding school discipline, then, represent a final step in the process of promoting student self-discipline. Such statements are written confirmation of the expectations of the school's hierarchy, its staff, the parent community, and the students themselves. Of themselves, such statements do not guarantee a well-ordered learning environment unless the school also relates them to its overarching values, models appropriate behavior, and promotes positive student/staff relationships. In this latter regard, the school that can turn heads by relating to students doesn't need to twist arms.

In essence, when the dean of students punishes someone for violating school policy, the school's rules and regulations may be affirmed, but the process of developing self-disciplined students has broken down somewhere. Don't get us wrong, certainly there are times when external discipline is required, even necessary to maintain a wholesome learning environment. Children are mischievous; adolescents are, by nature, counter-dependent. They require reasonable consequences for misbehavior.

The school hierarchy, however, that expects the development and enforcement of a student handbook to guarantee appropriate student behavior is as short-sighted as the administration that expects in-service training alone to improve the quality of instruction in the school. Like teachers who "own" their instructional improvement, students must "own" their appropriate behavior.

Schools that realize this provide collaborative opportunities for students, parents, and teachers to identify the values that will enable them to work together and to establish a cooperative and wholesome school environment:

+ They provide input opportunities for students, even dialogue groups during and after school to explore values generally and to share specific ideas about effective personal and school discipline.

+ They promote effective relationships among students and staff. The teacher, for example, who says to a student, "I'm sorry, but your language really makes me feel uncomfortable," does a better job relating to students and ultimately changing their behavior than the teacher who

says, "Tom, knock it off! Why do you have to be
such a jerk!"

These kinds of positive confrontational techniques for
teachers must be learned and periodically reinforced. They are
similar to the in-service training program for the improvement
of instruction. The information must be provided, and teachers
must have opportunities to integrate such techniques into their
daily behavior. "Discipline with dignity" is a guiding principle
for every adult in the building.

♦   Finally, maintain the school's focus on its norma-
    tive values. This is, perhaps, the primary respon-
    sibility of any school hierarchy that hopes to
    satisfy the personal and professional needs of
    students and staff.

Deerfield High School in Deerfield, Illinois, a school already
mentioned in this book, calls its program of school behavior
"FIRST CLASS" and sustains a focus on first-class behaviors,
congratulating students for their positive involvement in the
school and community and encouraging teachers to be sensitive
to students' feelings when encouraging appropriate behavior.
The program has met with considerable success and has been
copied by a variety of schools in the area. Here's how Thompson
Middle School in Pasadena, Texas, does it.

THOMPSON MIDDLE SCHOOL
PASADENA, TEXAS

COLLABORATIVE COMPONENTS

- Practices a "new way of organizing" that involves students and faculty in instructional decision-making
- Builds a shared vision of providing a quality world for all children based on commitment, cooperation and empowerment for all
- Incorporates the Total Quality Management process of Plan-Do-Study-Act in problem-solving
- Trains both faculty and students in quality process; parents and community are also involved
- Students learn in smaller, family-style teams that provide integrated learning
- Teachers devote two full, daily periods to planning and improving instruction

OVERVIEW

Thompson Middle School near Houston, Texas, boasts a diverse student body of over 1,000 students. Students and faculty together have created Total Quality Learning, Thompson-style! Against a setting for standards of excellence and equity for all children, students and teachers reflect on what is and what ought to be and plan instruction accordingly. Based on the quality concepts developed under the leadership of Dr. W. Edwards Deming, whose work was first embraced by Japan and later corporate America, learning at Thompson has undergone a distinct paradigm shift.

While many schools now use the quality process known as Plan-Do-Study-Act, few have such total involvement of students. Students engage mostly in project learning in teams of 125 to 160 that employ five core curriculum teachers of reading, writing, mathematics, science, and social studies. A competency matrix is used for each subject area, listing learning outcomes and elements of mastery that can be checked off as mastery is achieved. Grades are becoming "past tense" at Thompson because, as one student points out, the competency matrix tells you a lot more about what a student has learned and can do as a result of the learning.

PROGRAM HIGHLIGHTS

Important to the continuous improvement philosophy of learning is the time teachers devote to planning. Every day teachers work for two full planning periods, using the Plan-Do-Study-Act process to prepare and evaluate the learning experiences for children. It is recognized that if faculty leadership is truly valued, the critical element of time must be addressed.

Thompson's changing world began in the Fall of 1992, following an earlier TQM (Total Quality Management) workshop introduction hosted by the district. Attending that introductory conference was the principal, Vicki Thomas, the school counselor, and two teachers. Based on their joint experience, the group convinced the full faculty to look into the quality process which resulted in Thompson's very own adaptation. Initial training for faculty and students was a 3-day conference structure training experience that included ropes courses and highly interactive activities with names like "Punctured Drum Initiative," and "Team Walk."

In addition to teambuilding activities in which partici- pants learned the value of relying on each other, process tools used to measure improvement were also taught. Students and faculty learned how to use an affinity diagram, fishbone diagrams and Pareto charts as they went through the P-D-S-A (Plan-Do-Study-Act) process. All parties learned by practicing the process in every area of school life. That included planned learning experiences integrated through- out the subject areas as well as the all important social life of middle level students. Teachers report that conflict is now handled differently, and friendships emerge in a more respectful climate. Teachers report creativity, imagination and leadership are showing in all students, not just a few "stars."

The major difference in Thompson's flattened hierarchy is that students are the comanagers not only of their own learning, but of the school and its role in the community. This mindset taps into important developmental needs for early adolescents that have to do with service orientation and community responsibility. A real-life portfolio assessment that culminates in an eighth grade final rite of passage before an audience of family and friends is now a Thompson tradition.

THE PROCESS

The process starts with developing a shared vision, which in Thompson's case involved students, faculty, support staff, administration, parents, and community. The simply stated vision, providing a quality world for all children, is the hallmark for everything that follows.

A School Improvement Plan (SIP) is developed using the P-S-D-A process. A Thompson student describes the process:

First you have to discuss and look at the problem from many different eyes. This is in the first, or Plan, process. Because you have been trained in teambuilding, you know that you must rely on each other to understand and solve the problem. Everybody's viewpoint counts. Next you decide together what steps to take to solve the problem and you are in the Do part of the process. Next you Study what is happening (there are lots of tools to use) and discuss how to make it better. Then you Act on the changes. Sometimes they will be big changes and sometimes little adjustments and you can use how you problem-solved in other areas. Then you begin the process all over again.

Seven core committees are active in making sure the school vision and the SIP are working and improving:

- The Campus Improvement Plan is managed by the Campus Improvement team and includes peer elected members of the faculty, students, and parents.

- The Instructional Leadership Committee reviews progress of the action steps outlined in the School Improvement Plan (SIP).

- The Instructional Focus Committee oversees instructional support services and makes sure they are getting through for the benefit of all students.

- The High Expectations Committee works to support high standards and the belief that all students will learn.

- The Safe and Orderly Climate Committee makes sure that the learning environment is constantly improving.

- The Monitoring/Measurement Committee manages the data and big picture needed to view and communicate student achievement.

- The Parent and Community Support Committee ensures that strong links to the community are maintained and that school and community work together as one to build capacity for learning.

Tools of measurement, the continuous improvement theme of quality, and the emphasis on commitment, cooperation, and empowerment are the key components of Thompson's success. Every Thompson faculty member serves on one or more of the listed subcommittees. Again, the mindset for which they all strive is that all students will become quality producers.

WHAT CAN WE LEARN?

First and foremost, Thompson Middle School is yet another proven example of the successful implementation of a quality process. Most important, like other successful schools employing the quality process, they made it their own. Thompson's adaptation of Total Quality Learning is unique to their setting, and perhaps the most significant aspect of this Texas middle school is the program ownership of students and faculty as they work together.

Using teambuilding as a central training focus, new and creative approaches to learning, e.g., integrated curriculum, project learning, themes and portfolio assessment measures, were initiated. Results are showing at Thompson. Discipline referrals are down 45%, with fewer students being referred to the office and in-school suspension. Quality tool measures also show student conflicts are down and conflict resolution strategies are credited with helping students manage their own growth in this area. Test scores as measured by a state assessment procedure are up 10% schoolwide.

In 1993, Thompson was one of only 83 schools in Texas to be recognized and honored with a 5-year partnership with a Texas state education agency. This partnership includes funding opportunities as well as special workforce waivers that may be requested in the future.

Principal Vicki Thomas recently assumed the position of Director of Career Awareness and Technological Education at the Tegeler Career Center in this same Pasadena Independent School District. Her personal mission is the same: to bring the quality process to Tegeler, a high school, and to expand the involvement for quality learning in the district. Thomas' move to the high school underscores her confidence in the ability of faculty and students sustaining their shared vision of Thompson Middle School.

SCHOOL STATISTICS

Thompson Middle School
11309 Sagedowne Lane
Houston, Texas 77089

Grades: 6–8
Number of students: 1,000

Principal: Cheryl Fowler
Phone: 713/929–3850

8

COLLABORATIVE INPUT INTO SCHOOL POLICY

When asked whom he contacts first, the designer or the engineer, to deal with production problems, Lee Iacocca answered: "Neither. I talk to the person on the line. He or she works with the car every day and knows better than anyone else what needs to be done to correct the problem." He then went on to indicate that technical expertise belongs to the person who performs the job every day and that such persons are critical to the success of any enterprise.

Iaccoca is not the only successful leader to recognize the technical expertise of "the person on the line." Writers and practitioners in the field of educational administration have been promoting the technical expertise of classroom teachers for decades. From Chester Barnard's *Functions of the Executive* in 1938 and Douglas McGregor's *The Human Side of Enterprise* in 1960 to Thomas Sergiovanni's *Supervision: A Redefinition* in 1993, writers and practitioners have urged school systems to profit from the wealth of knowledge and experience that teachers bring to the job each day.

We have indicated elsewhere that schools have such a wide range of specialized responsibilities that no person or group of persons can be expected to be experts in all of them. For that matter, the body of pedagogical knowledge is expanding so rapidly and has become such an intricate combination of art and science that administrators can no longer be expected to be the only real experts in the classroom. Like Iaccoca, enlightened school administrators are now collaborating with teachers to improve the instructional and curricular processes. Such a reality leads us to:

> *Myth Number Thirteen:* "Because hierarchical responsibilities promote a view of 'The Big Picture,' school administrators are the logical persons to make most , if not all, of the school's instructional and curricular planning decisions."

Tradition would have us believe that such a statement is true. Perhaps some of it is, but its blanket acceptance obscures and devalues significant and essential input from teachers and others in the building. It is a statement rooted in the past, tragically out of touch with the significant changes that have taken place in our society. Most disturbing, it suggests behaviors that contradict commonly accepted theory, much of which has undergirded the teaching of educational leadership for decades.

THEORY REVISITED

Theory is so important to those of us who populate the halls of ivy that our students sometimes get tangled in the vines. Some of them never survive the experience. Life-sustaining to us, theory is often suffocating for them. We have always reasoned, however, that our search for collaboration in leadership will cause a few casualties. We much prefer to see a budding administrator die on the vine—than rot in the field.

Consider just one theory, the Getzels/Guba model of organizational relationships. No, we're not going to discuss the theory in its entirety. It probably has stretched your intellectual muscle to the breaking point already. We simply want to remind you that it consists of three dimensions: the institutional dimension (nomothetic) on the top, the individual dimension (idiographic) on the bottom, and the intermediate dimension (transactional) in the middle.

We want to remind you further that Getzels and Guba encouraged administrators to satisfy the needs of both the top and bottom dimensions equally and to do so by having the middle dimension promote an interplay between the two. Without such interplay, the theorists remind us, the maintenance needs of the institution and the human needs of individuals within it can come into conflict. In essence, administrators and teachers sometimes find themselves in adversarial positions.

Certainly this is no startling revelation. It is at this point, however, that the third dimension comes into play. It is the focus of this chapter. The organizational need to guarantee a predictability of behaviors within the school has resulted in a hierarchical ordering of responsibilities that often fails to accommodate the individual needs of teachers. SUPERVISION must fill the void. We believe that supervision is the third dimension in the Getzels and Guba model, the process that acts as the intermediary between the institution and the individual, that promotes collaborative decision-making.

Leadership, therefore, is multidimensional. It operates on the top dimension whenever administrators perform their traditional responsibilities and exercise hierarchical or expert authority. It operates in the middle dimension when department heads and others in supervisory positions act as intermediaries between the institution and the individual to assist each with the realization of their needs. It also operates on the bottom dimension whenever anyone other than an administrator or supervisor engages in the supervisory or administrative processes.

SUPERVISION AS A PROCESS

The school profiled in this chapter acknowledges collaborative input from teachers and recognizes that supervision is not a role occupied by a person or persons but a process that seeks out a wide range of individuals within the school. Teachers engaged in peer coaching have supervisory responsibility. Standing committees with terminal decision-making authorities have supervisory or administrative responsibility. Any time someone acts as an intermediary between the institution and the individuals within it, that person assumes a supervisory responsibility.

Supervision as a *role* necessarily restricts input from others in the school, many of whom have unique insights into building activities. Supervision as a *process* broadens the base of participation, involving a wider range of people to share ideas regarding professional growth and other planning activities. Prominent educator Art Costa says, "Intelligent people know what to do when they don't know what to do." We believe they put their faith in process.

The supervisory process, however, ceases to exist whenever those with supervisory responsibilities perceive themselves, or are organizationally defined, as "administrators." Administrators have a separate function in schools. They are charged, legitimately, with guaranteeing the survival needs of the system. Such a responsibility suggests that their role focuses on the top dimension of the Getzels and Guba model, a fact which often results in an unintentional disregard for the school's individual dimension.

Call such persons "upper-case Administrators." Supervisors, department heads, and other "middle-management" persons, when defined as "lower-case administrators," fail to assume the intermediate function in schools. They, too, perceive the institutional dimension as their exclusive focus. If no *supervisory* process exists within the school to act as the intermediary between the top and bottom dimensions, no one in the school's hierarchy is available to coordinate the school's needs with the teachers' needs.

An intermediate process within every school building is essential, therefore, if the institutional and the individual elements within it are to work collaboratively. This intermediate function—call it supervision—must operate in wide range of areas, each of which requires unique skills. We will discuss each of those areas generally at first, then look at some schools that have accommodated them specifically.

SUPERVISION REDEFINED

On the wide stage that is education, supervision, as distinguished from evaluation, has made only a recent appearance. It has grown from a bit player to a director, a backstage force that helps other performers look good. Education has benefited considerably from its appearance. As noted in Chapter 5, Woodrow Wilson indicated that judgment should provide light, not heat. Well, not only do classroom observations in some schools now replace heat with illumination, they actually eliminate the judgment. Many observations now emphasize teacher self-evaluation and define the supervisor as a peer. The resultant growth of collegiality has done much to replace hierarchical authority with expert authority and to emphasize the organizational as well as the individual benefits of teacher growth. We are grateful to Getzels and Guba for providing one of the conceptual frameworks within which such change could take place.

Many of us in the field are also grateful to such contemporaries as Art Costa, Bob Garmston, Carl Glickman, Noreen Garmon, Alan Glatthorn, and Madeline Hunter for extending the concepts of early thinkers like Getzels and Guba, Maslow, and McGregor into what is now a viable process of teacher supervision. As evidenced in Chapter 5, more and more schools across the country are complementing traditional teacher evaluation with formative experiences that promote improved professional performance. Supervision has come a long way within the past several years.

EXTENDING THE REDEFINITION

The time seems right to extend it even further, to look at it from yet another perspective. To do so, reconsider the two fundamental needs of any school: the needs of the institution to maintain itself and the needs of the people within it to find personal and professional satisfaction. As mentioned already, the two often conflict, particularly in schools that, for whatever reason, fail to provide a link between the organizational needs of the school and the human needs of the staff.

We like to call that link supervision, but in many of today's schools it involves a broader, more encompassing application of the helping relationship that now characterizes much of the literature. Supervision as a process now extends well beyond classroom observation. It has become the intermediary that helps teachers contribute to the normative values of the school while simultaneously satisfying their individual needs. It relates to all areas of the school's program—personnel, budgeting, program evaluation, curriculum, student behavior—as well as instruction.

Supervision has become so broad in its application that the term itself has several definitions. At one time synonymous with "evaluation," supervision has evolved into a helping relationship that enhances the professional growth of teachers. Now this helping relationship touches a wide range of organizational responsibilities and includes most of the staff. What the term has lost in semantic clarity, therefore, it has gained in practical application.

INCREASING SYNERGY IN SCHOOLS

First, a definition. *Webster's* defines synergy as, "the simultaneous action of separate agencies which, together, have greater total effect than the sum of their individual effects." Such synergistic effect can be dangerous, as when two otherwise harmless drugs combine to create a deadly effect. It can be positive as well, particularly in social institutions that combine individuals in collaborative activity.

Consider the words of Abraham Maslow:

> I shall speak of cultures with low synergy where the social structure provides for acts which are mutually opposed and counteractive, and cultures with high synergy where it provides for acts which are mutually reinforcing. . . . There are obviously institutions in our society which set us against each other, making us into rivals necessarily. . . . [Consider] the possibility of arranging social institutions . . . in such a fashion that the people within the organization are coordinated with each other and are perforce made into colleagues and teammates rather than into rivals.

In many schools the traditional emphasis on teacher evaluation has exacerbated the adversarial relationship between administrators and teachers. Additionally, the administration's predisposition to seek the goals of the school to the mutual exclusion of the needs of teachers in some sense has made them rivals. Mutual antagonism results in low synergy; the entire educational enterprise suffers. That this is happening in many schools across the country is well-documented in the media.

A variety of writers have addressed the issue, some in unique ways. Consider the thinking of Ann Wilson Schaeff, the author of *Women's Reality* and *When Society Becomes an Addict*:

> We are educated to be critical and judgmental. To be supportive and positive is viewed as being weak. This is especially evident in academia. . . . It is interesting—and frightening—to see how much defensiveness is a part of our culture. . . . When we live in a system that is compatible with and natural to the human species, a system that accepts us for who and what we are, then we have nothing to be defensive about. In that kind of system, all foibles and mistakes are opportunities for growth and learning.

THE COLLABORATIVE SYSTEM

We suggest that collaboration provides the essence of such a system. It promotes interrelationships which are much more "compatible with and natural to us," and, if organized like the programs that follow, it not only avoids judgment and criticism but promotes the kind of synergy that Maslow was seeking in all our social institutions. Fortunately, as evidenced in the next several pages, there are a great many schools out there that agree with us.

We must emphasize at this point that school administration is critical to the effective and efficient operation of schools. *Someone* has to guarantee the survival needs of the institution. This guarantee becomes a problem, however, when it operates to the exclusion of the human needs of everyone else in the school. The administrative *function*, therefore, must be complemented by a supervisory *process* that seeks to satisfy human and institutional needs simultaneously.

Much of the current thinking regarding supervision emphasizes collaborative planning and collegial interaction among all persons within the school, highlighting the perception that we are all partners seeking commonly shared and commonly accepted goals. The term "manager," therefore, doesn't deserve the negative treatment it has received in much of the literature.

Principals as "managers" perform a valuable function if they realize the importance of coalescing the knowledge and experience of the many leaders they find elsewhere in the building.

Concepts of supervision as a helping relationship and a process for promoting teacher autonomy and enhanced professional growth have had genuine impact on school systems. That these concepts extend beyond teacher observation and begin to influence all other areas of the supervisory relationship is education's next important step.

PATIENCE IS THE KEY

The first step may be the most difficult because it requires administrative willingness to break from traditional patterns of control. Administrators who are willing to take this first step must regard classroom teachers as colleagues and disregard expectations of deference and increased status within the school. Such administrators must perceive themselves as "teacher aides" and find their professional satisfactions not in the power or the status they receive from hierarchical position but in the relationships they establish and the achievements they promote in their teachers and students.

Additional steps will be equally difficult. As indicated elsewhere in this book, many teachers are conditioned by years of relative dependency to reject new opportunities to engage in school decision-making. Chris Argyris discovered years ago that the three-part cycle of managerial control, directive leadership, and hierarchical organization in most schools promotes dependency in teachers, which often results in their alienation.

At about the same time, researchers Alluto and Belasco found that collaborative decision-making ". . . may not be a viable administrative strategy for all segments of the school population." Their studies identified teachers within school systems who ranged from "decisional deprivation" to "decisional saturation." Older females, for example, tended to reflect saturation, young males deprivation.

Although these studies were conducted 20 years ago, the results are consistent with the experiences of administrators in schools across the country. Most practicing administrators realize that teachers seek different levels of decisional involvement. Some teachers desire a decrease in their levels of involvement, claiming, with some validity, that their primary responsibility is in the classroom and that any attempt to involve them in decision-making detracts from their teaching effectiveness.

Others, perhaps a majority, seek the decisional status quo, wanting simply to be "left alone" to teach their students and to enjoy the autonomy of their classrooms. Still others seek increased decisional authority, wanting, on the one hand, to influence the development of instruction and curriculum or, on the other, to find a way into the school's "inner circle," to prove their administrative mettle to possible sponsors in the school.

This latter reason warrants additional mention. Teachers either seek or avoid involvement in school decision-making for a variety of reasons, many of which are very subtle. They may avoid it because of their dissatisfaction with earlier and ongoing involvement with the school's hierarchy. Teachers sometimes feel manipulated during committee activity, resentful of controlling administrative behaviors, or powerless to influence their yearly assignments. Their dependency is well-documented in much of the literature; additional examples are unnecessary.

A result of this dependency, however, is their further alienation from the larger school system. As Argyris indicated decades ago, many teachers come to school to earn their salaries, to gain as much satisfaction as possible from their involvement with kids, and to leave immediately after the final bell, in essence to avoid additional involvement with the school in order to find their life's satisfactions elsewhere. Unfortunately, some of the best and most experienced teachers in the school fit this paradigm, which results in a significant loss to school planning activities.

Many of the younger teachers who seek decisional involvement enjoy it for the professional satisfaction it provides and for the opportunities it offers for advancement in the school system. This is both an advantage and a disadvantage to school administrators who want teachers to engage in collaborative planning activities. While such young teachers provide a willingness to involve themselves in collaborative planning, they fail to provide the breadth of experience of their veteran counterparts.

They also may seek involvement less to contribute collaboratively to the system and more to advance their own careers. Such teachers may, in effect, do more to perpetuate hierarchical organization and its unilateral decision-making than to contribute to the collaborative activity in the school. Short-sighted administrators who see this pool of teachers as an opportunity for collaborative planning may be involving the wrong persons for the job and inadvertently destroying collaborative concepts in their schools.

Administrators who intend to develop collaborative planning activities in their schools are well-advised, therefore, to identify the best persons in the building for the job and convince them of their indispensability, then to provide a broad range of educational experiences to prepare them for the difficult task of sharing their new decisional authorities. The following schools took the time to train their teachers for such responsibilities, recognizing that such a significant change in the daily routine of any teacher requires careful preparation.

We suggest, therefore, that schools interested in organizing similar programs spend adequate time training their staffs in the team-building skills that are so necessary to successful collaboration. The administrator who plans to implement collaborative activity "next month" or "at the end of the summer" is dooming the program to failure in his or her school. As indicated already, many teachers—maybe most—are unfamiliar with the skills involved in cooperative planning.

This may sound strange to those of us who read regularly of the cooperative learning that is finding its way into the nation's schools. In spite of the popularity of the term, however, it has not found its way into a majority of the nation's classrooms. Directed learning is as evident in these classrooms as directive management is in their schools' hierarchies.

Educators must not fall into the trap of implementing collaborative planning unilaterally. To do so is to envision it merely as a trend and not as a significant element in organizational redesign. The following programs at the Pierce Elementary

School in Fort Knox, Kentucky, are excellent examples of both the processes and the products of careful planning. At Pierce, the principal, teachers, and support staff make a team effort to grow continuously; they understand that team learning is an essential component in building their vision of a learning community.

PIERCE SCHOOL
FT. KNOX, KENTUCKY

COLLABORATIVE COMPONENTS:

+ Participatory leadership permeates the school climate
+ Trust and empowerment flourish among all participants, students, staff, parents and the broader community
+ Organizational structure based on team concept: TEAM—Together Each Achieves More
+ Continuous growth modeled by staff through peer coaching, activities that correlate with instructional improvement
+ Staff involved in every critical decision, e.g., hiring, planning, budgeting

OVERVIEW

Pierce Elementary School in Ft. Knox, Kentucky, serves military families with children in Kindergarten through third grade. Pierce's vision, "Empowered and united, our community, with unparalleled commitment, leads the way into the twenty-first century, creating the future through our students," is supported by a set of beliefs and core values that faculty and principal, Youlanda Washington work hard to bring alive for students, parents, and community. The staff is encouraged to model caring behavior and to teach leadership skills to their young students as a daily tool to learning. The idea of "leader among leaders" is designed to increase decision-making at the level where it is operating best and to encourage responsibility and team work for the entire organization.

The school year begins with an orientation for parents before the opening of school. This time is devoted to revisiting the school vision, explaining changes, and communicating expectations for the coming year. Seeking parent support is high on the Pierce agenda. When referencing the vision as a top priority, Washington believes that all parties must "catch the vision, and without it the people will perish."

The Pierce planning cycle begins with the annual retreat to review the direction and focus for the coming year. Teachers and principal together write the school improvement plan based on:

- School district goals
- School needs
- Recommended changes from parents and staff survey
- Recommended suggestions from staff

Organizational meetings are held by each team and team representatives once school has started. The clear purpose for these meetings is to organize team activities, review action plans and to move the process forward. Figure 8.1, which begins on page 166, is an example of a planning format.

Washington is among the newer principals in the district, now beginning her fourth year at Pierce. Her leadership style reflects her personal philosophy, "Kill all the dragons! Never pounce on the staff, build up one another through compassion and love. Always model kindness and let your character surface through integrity. People will follow leaders who demonstrate integrity." In her first 2 years, Washington, herself, sought the mentoring of a Ft. Knox colleague whom she considered to be an outstanding principal. Through his tutelage she quickly honed her leadership skills, and today this high school principal and elementary principal mentor each other. Both believe it is essential to have a trusted colleague that serves in a mentoring capacity. The modeling is also set for the peer coaching that is thriving among Pierce faculty.

THE PROCESS

As an outgrowth of the annual planning retreat, an organizational structure of teams, each with their own guidelines, move the process forward to accomplish the goals.

♦ *Cluster teams* are comprised of grade level teachers, students and support staff. They meet weekly and submit minutes to the principal. The cluster guidelines include managing organizational items, collaborating effectively to enhance teaching skills, discussions on how to assist learners and parents, planning team events to foster cooperation among students and engaging in creative ideas to support school focus.

♦ *Assessment teams* are currently involved in portfolio assessment, analysis teams (generates data as needed) and evaluation team (closely aligned with improvement plan.

♦ *Peer Coaching teams* meet on Wednesday mornings (no other meetings or conferences can be held on Wednesday morning) and often twice a week to discuss lesson plans, correlate activities, design projects, schedule observation times, discuss developmentally appropriate activities. This time is also set up for curriculum and assessment needs, e.g., scoring portfolios, reviewing curriculum information. Supervision at Pierce is tied to mutual support in accomplishing quality instruction for every child.

♦ *Committees* meet less often and, in general, carry out the tasks of planning and monitoring, and task accomplishments. Each committee has a symbol designating its responsibilities: advisory; decision-making; and both. For the 1995–96 school year, the following committees were in operation at Pierce:

Curriculum and Assessment, Staff Development, Technology, Guidance and Health, TAT (strategies for managing educational and behavioral needs of students, but not designed as a special education committee), Fine Arts, Opening Assembly (there is a morning assembly for all students each day to set school tone and enhance communication), Communication Council, Facilities, Grounds, and Maintenance, Red Cross and Social Committee, Interviewing (new personnel), Promotion (promoting school image), Program (discusses interest of community as it impacts school), and Team Representatives (discuss managerial issues, team concerns, review transformational plan "school improvement plan."

The above array of teams and committees may appear overwhelming to the reader, but to Pierce faculty and parents, it simply delineates the broad range of involvement and accomplishments expected for the coming year. For example, the Interviewing Committee meets only when there is a personnel opening and their task is to interview and recommend candidates that align with district and school's philosophy, mission, core values, and beliefs. The principal does not have a final vote. What distinguishes the operation of Pierce from other "participatory management" schools is the total trust and responsibility that is shared among faculty.

Another example of the process in action was when students were surveyed about their needs. Every child and parent was involved in the process; the number one item was new playground equipment. A committee reviewed all of the responses and a representative was selected from each class. From this experience the student body committee gained experience in writing, organizing committee meetings, and ordering materials. They made weekly reports to the entire school and during May the committee received over $10,000 worth of equipment.

Another feature of the communication process at Pierce was the development of the "rights and responsibilities" statement that appears with a preamble in the school handbook. As it states, "The wonder of living in democracy is the constant challenge of individuals expressing their rights while honoring and upholding their responsibilities." What follows are impressive lists of student rights and responsibilities, parent/guardian rights and responsibilities, faculty rights and responsibilities, and administration rights and responsibilities.

What distinguishes this school in implementing participatory decision-making is the total trust of faculty and staff to make autonomous decisions. The school theme or motto is "Caring Builds Success." Faculty, students, and parents take their responsibilities seriously and student achievement gains have confirmed their approach to learning. Figure 8.2, which begins on page 169, is an example of how parents can be involved.

WHAT CAN WE LEARN?

Principal Youlanda Washington knows when to lead and when to follow and support. She acts on her belief that staff and students must experience leadership development. Leadership books abound at Pierce and faculty are encouraged to read, read, read! She also believes that a school must operate first from its strengths. "Know your people. Match teams by strengths first, then identify weaknesses and develop a school plan to address them. Remember never to sacrifice your own principles nor allow staff to sacrifice theirs. Support risk-taking."

Like all of the schools profiled in this book, each is unique, but each was selected because their students are demonstrating that they are learning, and all are involved in changing to meet twenty first century needs. Pierce has the gifts of broad diversity of its military families and the challenge of students who come and go, who are rarely in the system for longer than two years.

The common thread of Pierce School, as demonstrated in all of the profiles, is a flattened hierarchy that supports true, collaborative leadership.

SCHOOL STATISTICS

Pierce School
7502 Dixie Street
Ft. Knox, KY 40121

Principal: Youlanda Washington
Phone: 502–624–7449

Number of students: 375
Grades: Kindergarten through grade 3

Number of faculty: 50 (including support staff)

FIGURE 8.1. SUGGESTED PLANNING FORMAT, PIERCE SCHOOL

COMPONENT: Discipline Plan   COMPONENT MANAGER: Principal   DATE

I. PROBLEM STATEMENT:
Lack of discipline process. Inconsistency in managing disruptive behaviors.

II. DESIRED OUTCOME (GOAL):
By 1996, the percentage of discipline problems would have decreased by 75%. All staff, students, and parents
would be able to explain the process. All staff would model and teach the appropriate behavior.
Staff behavior would be consistent with training series.

III ACTIVITIES	IV PERSON RESPONSIBLE	V DUE DATE	VI EVIDENCE OF ATTAINMENT, PRODUCTS, DELIVERABLES	VII RESOURCES NEEDED	VIII FUNDING SOURCE
1. During our school retreat, we would discuss discipline issues.	Staff	June 1994	Minutes from retreat	Consultant books, video tapes	Instructional budget. Ms. Jones $2,000.00
2. Create and implement plan	Staff	August 1994	Review document in Parent handbook, see each classroom for posting.		N/A
3. Develop supportive activities to enhance discipline plan. a. open assembly b. Wonderful Wednesdays (incentive program)	Counselor & Open Assembly Monitor	Sept. 1994	Review open assembly calendar 9/1994-1995 Review record of events	Books, activities, videos, guest speakers	$1,000.00 & P.T.O. donations
4. Develop teaching sessions through guidance department. Stage 2 of discipline plan a. staff training — staff teach skills that are identified	Counselor	March 1995	Review selected dates of presentation Review counselor's log Review open assembly booklet	Kits & videos	$750.00

COMPONENT: Discipline Plan (Page 2)   COMPONENT MANAGER: _____   DATE _____

I. PROBLEM STATEMENT:

II. DESIRED OUTCOME (GOAL):

III ACTIVITIES	IV PERSON RESPONSIBLE	V DUE DATE	VI EVIDENCE OF ATTAINMENT, PRODUCTS, DELIVERABLES	VII RESOURCES NEEDED	VIII FUNDING SOURCE
4. Stage 2 of discipline plan (cont'd) b. school wide training c. group guidance d. classroom guidance					
5. Evaluation of Plan	Analysis Team	June 1996	Review information at Summer Retreat	Documentation	$2,000.00 Pay for Retrea

COMPONENT: Communication   COMPONENT MANAGER: DATE:

I. PROBLEM STATEMENT:
All publics may not have felt informed about issues relating to Fort Knox Community Schools.

II. DESIRED OUTCOME (GOAL):
By 1996, effective communication to all publics

III ACTIVITIES	IV PERSON RESPONSIBLE	V DUE DATE	VI EVIDENCE OF ATTAINMENT, PRODUCTS, DELIVERABLES	VII RESOURCES NEEDED	VIII FUNDING SOURCE
(In House)					
• Panda Paws	Secretary	Daily	Staff mailboxes	Principal, Team Reps., Staff, Counselor, etc.	
• Menu a. Dates To Remember	Office Personnel	Weekly	Staff mailboxes Students/Parents Food Service Director	Food Service Director Dining Room Mgr. Principal, Staff	
• Newsletter a. new students b. events of two months c. birthday club d. student of the month e. dining room events f. school board meetings	Secretary	Monthly	Staff mailboxes Students/Parents School Board Director of Communications	Principal, Staff, Students, Director of Communications Opening Assembly Monitor (guest speakers)	

FIGURE FIGURE 8.2. PARENT VOLUNTEER ACTIVITIES

NAME_____ CHILD(REN'S) NAME(S) _____

ADDRESS_____   _____

PHONE_____

Please indicate one or more areas of interest for the parent(s) in your family. See description for each item below.

A ____ MULTI-CULTURAL PROGRAM   H ____ CROSSWALK/BUS STOP MONITOR

B ____ WONDERFUL WEDNESDAY   I ____ MINI OLYMPICS/FIELD DAY

C ____ ROOM PARENT -ROOM # ____   J ____ SPECIAL P.T.O. FUND RAISERS

D ____ LIBRARY/BOOK FAIR   K ____ GUIDANCE OFFICE ASSISTANCE

E ____ POPCORN COMMITTEE   L ____ PLAYGROUND EQUIPMENT INSTALLATION

F ____ SANTA'S WORKSHOP   M ____ PARENT ADVISORY BOARD

G ____ BOOK STORE   N ____ PROGRAM DESIGN GROUP

                                           O ____ GENERAL CLERICAL ASSISTANCE

A   Our P.E. Teacher stages a Multi-cultural program each spring. During the preparation period the various classes participate by studying the special Multi-cultural area assigned for the class.

B   Once a month a special activity will be provided for those students who have earned the privilege of attending such activities. Monitors are needed to help with the students at this time so that the classroom teachers may have a special planning period.

C   Parents are needed to help each classroom with various projects during the year. If you choose this area please indicate the room number of your child where indicated.

D   The Library hosts 2/3 Book Fairs each school year at which parental help for our student shoppers would be helpful. The Library can also use assistance in shelving books or general library duties during the year.

E   The PTO Popcorn Committee sells popcorn to the students every other Friday. Help is needed to pop the corn, bag it, and distribute it to the classrooms.

F   Santa's Workshop, operated each fall by the PTO, can use parents as sales assistants to our student shoppers.

G   Last year the PTO operated a "Book Store" on Monday, Wednesday and Friday during the morning assembly period. General school supplies were available for purchase at that time.

H   Crosswalk/Bus Stop Monitors are a great safety factor in preventing accidents when our students come to or depart from school.

I   Our P.E. Teacher hosts a Mini Olympics/Field Day near the end of school each year. Volunteers are needed to judge races and award ribbons.

J   During the school year the Pierce PTO stages several fund raisers, such as the candy sale held in early fall. Parents are needed during various stages of these projects.

K   Our Guidance office maintains the Birthday Club and Student of the Month selections each month. Help is needed to create bulletin boards and name tags for these events.

(continued on reverse side)

L   New playground equipment has been received by Pierce School and the old equipment needs some re-furbishing. Fathers are needed to assist our Custodians in erecting the new equipment and sand blasting and re-painting the old.

M   The Parent Advisory Board assists the Principal in resolving any problems that might arise during the school year.

N   The Program Design Group helps the Principal to evolve new programs which will enhance the curriculum of Pierce School.

O   General clerical assistance is needed by many departments here at Pierce at various times during the school year. Example: Assembly of the school newsletter which is sent out each month.

IF YOU HAVE ANY QUESTIONS ABOUT ANY OF THESE AREAS OF INTEREST PLEASE FEEL FREE TO CALL THE SCHOOL OFFICE AT 624-7449.

REFERENCES

Alutto, Joseph A., and Belasco, James A. 1972. Patterns of Teacher Participation in School System Decision-Making. *Educational Administration Quarterly*, pp. 27–39.

Argyris, C. 1960. Individual actualization in complex organizations. *Mental Hygiene*, 44(2): 226–37.

Getzels, J. 1968. *Educational Administration as a Social Process*. New York: Harper and Row.

Maslow, A. 1954. *Motivation and Personality*. New York: Harper and Row.

Schaeff, A.W. 1987. *When Society Becomes an Addict*. New York: Harper and Row.

9

EDUCATION'S HIERARCHY AND THE NEED FOR CHANGE

Almost 100 years ago, George Bernard Shaw asserted, in *Man and Superman*, that "change is an illusion." If the survival rate of education's trends is any indication, Shaw was undeniably correct. Consider the parade of trends, some quite well-conceived, that came and went—and then came and went again. Some trends have shifted the building blocks of what we do, but none has provoked an elaborate reconstruction of our jobs and workplaces. Several have provoked compromises, the kind that result not in changes in the school's primary programs but in the development of ancillary programs that promote the appearance of change.

Changes rarely occur within the primary programs in most schools. Curricula, methods of instruction, organizational arrangements, decision-making processes, and delivery of services to students have remained fundamentally the same in schools within the past several decades. Consider, as just one example, the study skills that students require to succeed in different curricula.

Study skills in geography are different from those in algebra. Studying an American literature anthology is different from conducting a biology lab experiment. Study skills are so critical to learning that the subject recently received broad examination in the literature. Did it provoke widespread change in the schools? Did it encourage a majority of teachers to include time in their classrooms to give students the skills they need to master their subjects?

Perhaps in some, maybe even in many; certainly not in all, not even in most. Several conscientious teachers read the articles and books and did what they could to work more closely with their students to improve their study skills. Most disregarded the information and proceeded with business as usual. A few immersed themselves in the information, recognized it as an important solution to an obvious need, introduced needed changes in their classrooms, and even developed ancillary programs for their schools.

Their administrators applauded these teachers because the programs were consistent with the literature and highly relevant. They pumped a few dollars into the programs, gave one or more teachers released time to coordinate them, and invited students to seek out these teachers when they needed help with their study skills. Some schools even encouraged teachers to refer students for specific help.

CHANGE REMAINS AN ILLUSION

Having done so, such schools pat themselves on the back and stake their claim to the forefront of American education. And not one person in any one of them recognizes that the new programs are little more than an expression of an unresolved problem in the school's primary program. The students who really need help with their study skills rarely refer themselves, and the teachers who should be teaching study skills in their classrooms now feel they don't have to—because of the program.

At this point, the study skills program has become a part of the problem. So it is with many, maybe most, ancillary programs in schools. Their existence responds to a need but doesn't resolve it, except in the minds of the teachers and administrators, who are convinced that study skills have been accommodated. Such self-deception regarding ancillary programs simply underscores Shaw's perception.

EDUCATION'S NATURAL RESISTANCE TO CHANGE

Systems theorists may think Shaw's belief extreme, but they acknowledge that systems, by definition, are resistant to change. The reasons are understandable. Systems develop steady states that seek only the status quo. It follows, then, that schools find it easier to develop ancillary programs than to change the primary system. Department chairs and administrators, therefore, must ask themselves a few important questions when involved in program planning:

♦ Who supports this program?

♦ Why do they support it?

♦ Exactly what does it do? What problem(s) does it resolve?

♦ What experiences are provided by this program?

♦ Do these experiences extend, modify, or replace elements in the school's primary program?

This last question is the most critical. The answer to it helps determine if curriculum, instruction, or school organization are being affected. Then planners must ask, "If they are not being affected, should they be?" If the problem exists in the primary program, most of it should be resolved in the primary program. That's perhaps the biggest irritation when identifying problems. Someone inevitably expects us to do something about them. Unfortunately, many schools have discovered that the easiest way to do that is with an ancillary program.

CHANGE IS STILL NEEDED

It is not the best way. An ancillary program to assist students with their study skills probably doesn't affect the majority of students, certainly not the majority of those who most need the help. Similarly, ancillary programs involving collegial supervision for teachers may or may not be functionally integrated within the professional development activities of the entire staff. If they are not coordinated with evaluation and in-service training, they probably won't influence the instructional strategies of teachers who most need the help. Again, at this point, the ancillary program is less a solution for the problem and more an indication of the problem itself.

Consider yet another example. An ancillary tutoring program for low-achieving students often gives tacit permission for teachers to leave immediately at the end of the school day. An ancillary study skills program gives tacit approval to teachers to disregard the topic in the classroom, where it is most needed and when it can be presented to every student. An ancillary peer supervision program gives supervisors and administrators tacit encouragement to emphasize evaluation over formative supervision with teachers. A writing resource center for students gives tacit approval to teachers in all subject areas to disregard planned instruction on writing skills. And so it goes.

Each of us, therefore, must ask ourself to what extent the development of ancillary programs signals problems within the school's primary program, in essence, what actually happens in classrooms and counselors' offices. Then we must ask the tough questions. Should we find more time during the day, possibly after school, for teachers to tutor students? How do we incorporate study skills into classroom instruction? How do we emphasize study skills across the school's curriculum?

How can supervisors work more closely with collegial groups and individual teachers to assure their formative growth? Without the knowledge and focus of answers to such questions, schools everywhere will expend their efforts only on the periphery of substantive change, and they will allow the critics of education to continue shooting at stationary targets.

Myth Number Fourteen: "The hierarchy is the primary force that maintains the roles and responsibilities for accommodating the adaptive needs of the school."

Often, the exact opposite is true. That's what this chapter is about—making substantive change in the school's primary program. Much of this book has emphasized, for example, that if the hierarchy is getting in the way of substantive change, modify it and seek the collaborative involvement of others who can avoid the illusion of change and promote the kinds of altered programs that meet the real needs of students and teachers.

CHANGE AS REACTIVE OR PROACTIVE

Change is inevitable. Adaptive reactions characterize every system, especially schools, which are subject to conflicting social pressures and changing professional opinions. Responses to such pressures for change can be reactive, proactive, or *inactive*. If systems are inactive when the forces for change are greater than the forces for the status quo, the resultant random changes affect systems in unpredictable and sometimes destructive ways.

Reactive change is often as bad. Such reactions generally result from a fragmented perception of the purposes of the system. Many school hierarchies focus on the survival strategies needed to maintain the school's and their own vested interests. While this may help maintain the school, it provokes an inability to see the "Big Picture," to see the school as an entire system, and to understand the interrelationships within that system that bring it to life and that may require periodic revitalization.

Reactive change in schools is the sporting equivalent of playing the Dallas Cowboys without a game plan, without assessing their strengths and weaknesses and making strategic changes to improve the team's chances for victory. Proactive planning makes such changes by anticipating the adaptive needs within the system. Unfortunately, many schools, maybe most, are notoriously poor planners.

This may be true for several reasons, all of which relate to the hierarchy in one way or another:

♦ All school systems work with a *deserved*, as opposed to an *earned*, budget. The service or product developed by schools, in most instances, defies accountability. Politicians, educators, and others have been seeking accountability in the nation's schools for decades and have yet to see it take hold. Most schools continue, therefore, to receive predictable yearly budgets and to curry the favor of the local community through public relations activities to periodically increase annual budgets.

Budgetary increases, therefore, relate not as much to the quality of education's product as to the intensity of its public relations efforts. Certainly, some schools point to National Merit Scholars and average ACT scores as evidence of academic excellence, and, to some extent, these are appropriate criteria. In most instances, however, such standards of excellence relate more to the quality of the student with whom they work than the superiority of the instructional program.

♦ School hierarchies are as concerned as much with their own personal survival as with the survival of the system itself. Ambrose Bierce once described politics as "the conduct of public affairs for private advantage." The media underscore such a definition of governmental politics every day. Such a definition is equally appropriate for education and business, not that school administrators defraud the public of school funds or yield to the expectations of lobbyists, but that they maintain internal processes that favor their positions.

Sometimes these internal processes avoid change. In fact, teachers everywhere are familiar with school administrators who implicitly encourage teachers not "to make waves," often to the point of accepting mediocrity in the classroom if teachers do their jobs with a minimum of student misbehavior or parent complaint. Such an administrative predisposition obviously favors the status quo and disregards the fundamental needs of the system.

♦ This leads to a consideration of the growing opinion in much of the literature that teachers and administrators don't necessarily fear *change* as much as they fear *being* changed. Both administrators and teachers come to accept a school's cultural pattern of interpersonal relationships, the predictability of its routine, its policies governing behavior, and its processes for curricular and instructional improvement.

Different ways of doing things often causes teachers as well as administrators to adjust their own behavior and to operate in ways that are inconsistent with their social and psychological comfort levels. A change to collaborative leadership, for example, requires that administrators learn to dialogue and to share the decisional process with others in the building or the community. Such an expectation is foreign to many practicing administrators and can provoke resistance.

Similarly, many teachers who are suddenly expected to participate in the collaborative search for curricular or instructional improvement tend to perceive such involvement as an imposition on their time, a diversion from classroom activities. If they are inadequately compensated for such additional time, they, too, tend to become resistant.

♦ Decades ago, Max Abbott, then the dean of the College of Education at Auburn University, delivered a graduation speech in which he discussed the "hierarchical impediments to innovation in educational organizations." Among the many characteristics he described, perhaps the most obvious was the hierarchy's successive layers of control, any one of which can veto a promising idea, thereby inhibiting change. Said Abbott:

> Such a system obviously favors the status quo and inhibits innovation from below. Yet, in an organization which consists largely of professionals, as is the case in

an educational institution, meaningful and workable innovations almost necessarily originate at the lower levels of the hierarchy.

As indicated elsewhere, teachers possess the technical skills that are most important in the classroom. Certainly, they can refine these skills with the assistance of knowledgeable and sensitive supervisors and colleagues. The point is, their daily interaction not only with students but with the curriculum and the teaching/learning process gives them insights into needs within the system that may not be as obvious to members of the hierarchy.

♦ The problem is further complicated by a phenomenon we call the *"Sunshine Syndrome."* The attempts of some administrators to develop a sense of family and a favorable self-perception sometimes result in the inability to be self-critical. They are so predisposed to tell each other how wonderful they are that they obscure shortcomings in the building. This is yet another of the ways that "steady states" are maintained in schools.

The "Sunshine Syndrome," therefore, both binds and blinds. On the one hand, it promotes the sense of family that binds people together with a common sense of purpose; on the other, it blinds individuals to the faults of the organization and inhibits the problem-solving processes that are so important to needed change. Whereas it develops the managers who are needed to sustain the maintenance and survival needs of the organization, it fails to create the leaders who provoke the self-criticism that is so essential to improvement.

If Daniel Griffiths was correct so many years ago when he said that an "optimal divergency" must exist in organizations to assure needed change, blind identification with an idealized school is potentially destructive—to the administration as well as to the school. Such is one of the traditional problems with the hierarchy. To improve, schools must establish the processes that value and develop the leaders within the school that promote periodic soul-searching.

Collaborative processes must engender in school administrators a willingness to break from the desired predictability of the hierarchy in order to secure the input of those others who ask unpredictable but essential questions of the school. Such an organization may be hierarchical in design, but, in application, it promotes collaborative processes that nurture the seeds of its own growth.

♦ Change in many schools is further inhibited by the hierarchy's tendency to perceive the change process as a straight line, from the identification of a problem on one end of the continuum to the implementation of a solution on the other. We suggest that the change continuum, however, is best illustrated as a circular rather than a straight line. See Figure 9.1.

Schools that perceive the change continuum as a straight line generally identify or assume a problem, then identify one or more solutions to resolve it. Such solutions are assumed successful or unsuccessful, depending on the apparent resolution of the problem. If the solution isn't successful, some schools attribute it to teacher resistance and either disregard the problem or seek another solution.

FIGURE 9.1. PERCEPTIONS OF CHANGE

Traditional Perception of Change

Problem   Solution

CHANGE PROCESS

Improved Perception of Change

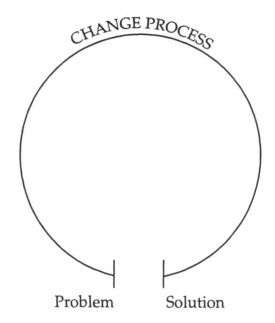

CHANGE PROCESS

Problem   Solution

Rarely do schools monitor the progress of solutions in order to determine the relative degree of their success or to make adjustments in their performance. Schools that acknowledge the planning continuum as cyclical, as in Figure 9.1, monitor solutions and regard their failure as the identification of another problem, one that might be responsive to slight adjustments in the original solution or that might require alternatives.

In essence, such schools evaluate the performance of all solutions, determine the relative degree of their success, and resume planning activities when it becomes apparent that they aren't doing what they were designed to do. The planning process, therefore, is ongoing. It identifies continuing problems as well as new ones and responds with new or periodically adjusted solutions. As suggested in Figure 9.1, therefore, the gap between a problem and its solution is a small one in order to promote the continuing adjustments solutions require for success.

♦ Finally, all these characteristics of the school hierarchy result at times in a "bandwagon approach" to change. Schools are dependent on a satisfied community for continued financial support. The community that values education and aggressively supports its schools expects to see improvement in curricular and instructional activities. In the absence of time-consuming and, occasionally, complicated planning activities, schools often provide evidence of improvement by incorporating prominent trends in the school program.

Most of these trends are prominent in the professional literature and are presented so convincingly that some schools implement them with little regard for the problems they are seeking to resolve. In essence, some schools implement trends with little regard to preliminary planning activities, fostering a "monkey see, monkey do" approach that involves prepackaged solutions to poorly defined problems. Then, many administrators wonder why they don't work.

Short-sighted administrators blame teacher resistance for the failure of the new program, and the status quo is effectively reaffirmed. Change, then, remains an illusion, the reasons found somewhere in the hierarchy's inability to plan effectively, not in the staff's unwillingness or inability to accept change. Schools sometimes forget that a clear assessment of current practice is as important as a vision for the future.

MORE ABOUT TRENDS AND THE CHANGE PROCESS

Trends are to education what rookies are to professional sports—exciting but unfulfilled promises. Unlike rookies, however, trends are expected by the veterans among us to be short-lived. As such, they generally fail to receive the kind of help they need to transform potential into actual success. They generally come and go, appear in an explosion of expectation, and almost as quickly disappear.

And some of them are good. The changes they suggest for education are sorely needed in some schools and are generally based on years of research and planning. Why, then, are some trends welcomed so gleefully at birth, neglected so obviously during infancy, mourned so little after death, and resurrected so blindly 20 years later? The answer must have something to do with the systems that are supposed to nurture them.

It's important to recognize that many trends are little more than the continuing attempts of the profession to resolve inconsistencies in practice. As a profession, for example, we purport to value the autonomy of teachers and the need for their involvement in the school's decision-making processes. Twenty years ago, shared decision-making and participative management suggested ways to make this happen; recently "teacher empowerment" did the same thing. Twenty years from now another concept/trend may emphasize the same things and perhaps be just as unsuccessful as past and current ideas.

Trends not only foster change, they require an environment with the ability and the willingness to change. Their survival depends on it. An unshakable status quo is deadly to trends. It is the organizational equivalent of suffocation. Educational leaders must look critically at the systems within which they operate to identify elements that seek the status quo. If one of these elements is the hierarchy, particularly as discussed by Abbott, they must modify it to accommodate needed change.

THE ELEMENTS OF COLLABORATIVE PLANNING

Collaborative planning presumes that most principals accept the notion that the school, with one trifling exception, is composed of others. When these others engage in collaborative planning with members of the hierarchy, the system's need for predictability is diminished by the sheer force of differing opinion. Effective collaborative planning, therefore, reflects Charles Caleb Colson's belief that "we owe almost all of our knowledge not to those who have agreed with us but to those who have differed."

Good administrators, like good coaches, learn early in their careers that if every member of a staff of 10 coaches agrees all the time, nine of them are unnecessary. Such administrators realize the value of conflicting opinion as well as the synergy that results when administrators, teachers, students, and parents engage in the dialogue that promotes collaborative exploration of the school program and a shared perception of desirable improvements.

Differing opinions may be dangerous to administrators who seek the status quo, but they are essential to substantive change in schools. Consider the fact that the Chinese character for crisis contains two elements—one expresses danger, the other, opportunity. We have indicated already that most changes suggest both. How we react to that fact, however, determines the effect of change on us and our schools.

If we learn to manage change by anticipating it and promoting collaborative responses, we become its master instead of its victim. We learn, for example, to anticipate needed change, to read the signs of incipient problems. Something within the environment is causing:

- Obvious instability, even chaos.
- Increased conflict.
- Higher levels of stress
- Administrative fear of a loss of control.

There may be other signs as well, but these suggest that something is wrong in the system and that planning is necessary to determine the exact implications of the problem. In essence, appropriate planning begins with an assessment of the current situation, with a discrepancy analysis of the difference between "what is" and "what should be." This is a critical step and must involve all representatives of the system in order to develop a complete picture.

According to Roger Kaufman, in his book *Educational System Planning*, successive steps in the planning process involve:

- The determination of solution requirements and solution alternatives. In other words, how do we want future solutions to perform?
- The selection of solution strategies from among a variety of alternatives.
- The implementation of selected strategies to realize desirable outcomes.
- The determination of performance effectiveness. In other words, are the solutions doing what they were designed to do? This is the monitoring process referred to earlier.
- Necessary revision of any step in the process to resolve the problem.

This final step suggests that the process is, in fact, cyclical and that the identification of new or continuing problems in the system requires a planning process that is ongoing. Implicitly, it also suggests that everyone in the system must be represented or actually involved in the process to assure the self-criticism that leads to the effective identification of problems and the success of solution elements. Collaboration, therefore, is critical in any school planning activity.

Collaboration also promotes the social interaction that enables school leaders to deal with the anxiety which is inevitable during the change process. Change normally involves movement from relative comfort and certainty to discomfort and uncertainty. Persons in the system may require extra support in developing the new behaviors that result in successful change. Change, therefore, is a process, not an event and is best facilitated in a setting that promotes dialogue and social interaction.

THE RELATIONSHIP OF HIRING TO CHANGE

Given the changing decision-making practices in many schools, administrators must no longer emphasize only the academic records of prospective teachers. Our experience indicates that growing numbers of schools are seeking candidates with the ability to self-criticize, interact socially and professionally with colleagues, look beyond their classrooms in order to understand the total school system, reflect and explore issues collaboratively with other teachers, and think independently.

The skills involved in successful collaboration can be taught and, as such, should be incorporated into orientation programs for new teachers. The predispositions to collaborate, however, are often another issue and should be incorporated into the hiring criteria for all candidates during the interviewing and selection processes. In addition, the hiring of collaborative teachers is best accomplished *collaboratively*. Following, then, are a few suggested practices:

- ♦ Recruitment and Screening
  Meet with members of the department, students, and even parents to determine the needs that this person will be expected to satisfy. This aspect of hiring suggests only one of several

reasons why hiring corresponds so closely to school planning. Does the school need a biology or a chemistry teacher, a person who eventually will be expected to fill the shoes of the current AP teacher, an advocate of collegial supervision, or someone who can "fit" within the school and community culture?

Teachers, students, and parents can answer these kinds of questions better than anyone else. Their involvement in this initial phase of recruitment not only helps describe the person the school is seeking but gives everyone a sense of ownership in the process. Many of these same people may be involved in the actual interviewing process and will bring to that responsibility a detailed knowledge of what the school is seeking. Generally, the initial screening of candidates is done by someone in the administrative hierarchy, but everyone else in the school can feel comfortable that they had some input into the actual screening process.

◆ Interviewing

Administrators must be careful to structure the interviewing format. They must provide evidence of the kinds of questions that interviewers can and cannot ask, who will be doing the interviewing, the criteria to use to evaluate each candidate, and what processes to follow when the interviews have been completed.

Obviously, interview committees must be used, but they must regard the interview as only one part of the selection process. Subjective assessments are important, but they are especially effective when complemented by objective information such as biographical information, letters of reference, and reference checks by phone.

Finally, be sure to encourage everyone involved in the process to maintain written records. Good records maintain first impressions and serve to remind interviewers of important information. They also provide valuable documented information if legal action results from the rejection of a candidate.

♦ Selection Process

The candidate who is selected as a result of the process is the solution to your problem. As such, this person must be carefully monitored during his or her first few years to determine if the original need as identified by you and your staff has been satisfied. If not, the problem must be resolved by closely supervising the new teacher or by seeking other candidates and resuming the hiring process.

Hiring good teachers is but one element in the total planning process for schools. As with all good planning, it is ongoing and engages everyone in the system in collaborative activity. It gives everyone not only a sense of involvement but a strong feeling of ownership for the solutions that result from the planning. Obviously, some schools manage change and the planning process better than others. The Waggoner Elementary School in Tempe, Arizona, has followed a studied, carefully orchestrated approach to site-based management. It is an excellent example of a school choosing its own path for improvement.

WAGGONER SCHOOL
TEMPE, ARIZONA

COLLABORATIVE COMPONENTS

♦ Employs a site-based management model that differs from most; decision-making responsibility is divided among several groups

♦ Parents are a part of the major decision-making processes and take responsibility for their own continuing education about Waggoner

♦ District support in the form of leadership training and latitude for every school to chart own course

♦ Long-term strategic plan maps improvement goals and assessment

♦ Pays attention to systems feedback through use of pyramid structure

OVERVIEW

Arizona's Kyrene School District has been recognized for its futuristic management of change and site-based management. Long before the recent state mandate for site-based management statewide, Kyrene invested in training for Total Quality Management, systems thinking, shared decision-making, and strategic planning, to name several. What resulted, according to Bob Hedsel, Assistant Superintendent, is a creative combination of approaches that allow each school to be different, although held to high standards of performance.

Kyrene also partners with one of the big names in the corporate world, Intel Corporation, which shares the goal of a community-based systemic structure. Intel's contribution of Management by Planning arose from the corporate giant's rejection of its application for the prestigious Baldridge

Award. In its critique, the Baldridge committee noted that Intel was doing all of the right things, but in the final analysis, nothing connected. In response, Intel created Management by Planning which added emphases in integrating their multiple assessment measures and new methods of formative assessment.

Interaction Associates of San Francisco (also used by Intel for training) helped the district organize multiple plans and create the education version of Intel's Management by Planning. At present there are seven in-district trainers who hold "facilitator licenses" from Interaction Associates.

Waggoner School, the oldest in the district, was the first to look into site-based management. Calling it "collaborative decision-making," principal Julie Weimer was encouraged by the central office to explore the ideas and philosophy with faculty and parents during the Spring of 1991.

Recalling this period, Weimer remembers that she and the faculty spent an entire year writing their SIP (School Improvement Plan) and setting goals. The first group to be formed in the Fall of 1991 was the Management Team, comprised of seven teachers, four parents, and the principal. There was a gradual introduction of the Parents' Forum team the following January, and soon after, the Curriculum Committee, which makes instructional decisions, and the Liaison team comprised of school staff members that handle day-to-day decision-making, e.g., recess time, and scheduling modifications. In addition to these groups, a PTO parent group functions as part of the educational process that provides a service orientation.

PROGRAM HIGHLIGHTS

What makes Waggoner's model different from others is that while the Management Team guides the "big picture," the other groups are fairly autonomous and make important decisions in their area of responsibility.

A pyramid structure for communication provides the critical connecting link. The principal is a member of every group except the curriculum group which is the action component of the School Improvement Plan.

The Management Team differs from the Liaison Team and the other groups, not only in areas of responsibility which include staffing issues, policy, budget, etc., but in how it operates. Lots of time is spent in educating the group on important issues on the agenda at hand, plus those that are likely to be addressed in the future. The key difference is in anticipating future needs and directions. Decisions are made in a deliberative mode.

The Liaison Team's meeting style is totally different, fast paced, and usually dealing with issues, challenges and obstacles to creating smooth operations in a positive environment.

The Parent Forum, meeting once a month on issues, is run by the parent members of the Management Team. The principal and/or teachers are often invited to provide information and make presentations, but the agenda is very much owned by the parent group.

The Curriculum Committee is comprised of a group of teachers who commit to working together for 3 years (the length of the School Improvement Plan) and is essentially autonomous in its operation. This group, however, recognizes and responds to its responsibility to communicate with other groups. The interdependency of the system was demonstrated when the science committee subgroup made a decision to incorporate a "scientist in residence" program. Both the Management Team and the PTO parent organization who would help fund the program were involved early in the decision process.

The PTO parent organization, unlike the Parent Forum group who deals with hot issues, provides a service orientation as well as a parent education component. Currently, there are projects to bring art into the classroom and "family math nights" or "family science nights" that help parents understand and develop their tutoring, facilitating role in the education process.

The pyramid structure for communication is designed around grade levels that include special areas and special programs. Both informal and formal methods of communication are used—there are published (usually 1 page) minutes from every meeting that are color-coded and circulated to make it easy for everyone to "keep up." People remind each other (often in humorous ways) to take responsibility for reading the written communication. Because teachers are so used to working together, no one says, "That's nice for you, but here's what I'm going to do."

The Waggoner model for making decisions is their systems framework which they strengthen each year by creating and trying new links for systems interdependence. In this way, they connect with the district and with the larger community.

THE PROCESS

In describing the process at Waggoner, principal Julie Weimer credits her husband, John Weimer, a principal in nearby Scottsdale, Arizona, who is a recognized trainer on skill-building needed for successful, long-term shared decision-making. John Weimer helped the Waggoner groups write their School Improvement Plan and led earlier training sessions on effective meeting skills and site-based decision-making process. Training in teambuilding is also ongoing.

Weimer's own growth as a facilitative leader has been enhanced by leadership training from Interaction Associates whose other customers include Apple, Intel, and other major businesses. She makes the point that leadership must be shared responsibility and that the principal as a facilitator cannot always be neutral.

Change does not come without its challenges, both for individuals and groups. In the first years of change, several faculty elected to leave Waggoner. As principal Weimer explained to her faculty, "We have made a joint decision to create and follow our own model for collaborative decision-making. If you cannot thrive in this setting, I pledge to assist you in finding one where you can grow and develop."

Groups, too, are different and these differences contribute to growth. The first Management Team at Waggoner was extremely futuristic, looking ahead and trying to be pro-active. This year's Management Team prefers to deal more with "the here and now, the nitty gritty." Then there was a Parent Forum several years ago that erupted into shouting and accusations over a hot issue that was being debated. "I learned from that experience," says Weimer, "to always state, 'I believe', instead of 'I feel.' It is important for educational leaders to be up front with their beliefs and to state them clearly."

Waggoner's progress over the last 4 years also reflects Weimer's leadership style, persistent, low-key, and facilitative. Weimer encourages all of the stakeholders to educate themselves and the group on all issues. As a result of a more deliberative pace, people have become more and more involved. This past school year, cooperative learning was a major instructional push. This coming year, Waggoner will concentrate on alternative assessment. The systems framework of collaborative decision-making and the autonomy afforded under site based management provides an effective support mechanism.

WHAT CAN WE LEARN?

From Waggoner School in the Kyrene District in Arizona, we see a district that supports and encourages schools to be different and to have ownership of the important decisions. Assistant Superintendent Hedsel admits, however, that the toughest part of changing is to figure out (from the central office perspective) how schools can be different and in what ways they should be alike. In Kyrene, the current strategy is to encourage and support many different paths to achievement and to provide assessment standards, not assessment procedures.

We also learn that patience and persistence in helping teachers and parents in the change process provides a steady momentum for progress. Waggoner divides responsibilities and decision-making authority among several groups, depending upon a pyramid structure of communication to keep people informed and involved where necessary.

Waggoner also provides a model for changing the hierarchy in an established, "oldest in the district" school setting. It is a tribute to the parents and faculty that they did not rely on the often repeated adage, "If it isn't broken, don't fix it." Before and after their significant change, Waggoner School's student achievement scores remain the district's highest.

School Statistics

Waggoner Elementary School
1050 E. Carver Road
Tempe, AZ 85284

Grades: K through 5
Number of students: 550
Minority representation: 10%

Principal: Julie Weimer
Phone: 602/496-4733

10

EDUCATION'S HIERARCHY: ITS LIKELY FUTURES

First, a quick story: Years ago, when Mike, one of the authors of this book, was a fledgling administrator, he was asked by the principal to chair a committee of teachers and administrators to explore education's most intriguing new trend, variable modular scheduling. A consultant to the district had visited the previous summer and had extolled the virtues of flexible schedules, leaving the superintendent and the building principals fired with the desire to study the concept further.

Mike agreed to chair the committee and convened his group early in the school year. Seeking background information and because the principal was an *ex officio* member of the committee, Mike asked him at the first meeting why they were studying the concept. The principal responded with the comment, "Why do you always have to ask why?" He then asserted that variable modular scheduling was education's hottest new topic and that it might relieve some of the school's scheduling pressures. "Is that a good enough reason?"

Fledgling administrators learn to live with such aggressive enlightenment from their principals, so they got on with the meeting and launched the committee on a year-long study of variable modular scheduling, which included visits to neighboring schools, extensive research, and the development of an informational booklet for each member of the faculty. At the end of the year, the committee decided to distribute the booklets at a faculty meeting, provide additional information, and answer questions.

Everyone in the committee assumed that the principal would lead the faculty meeting, but he declined, indicating that if *he* led it "there is no way the faculty will go along with the idea." Mike was elected. The meeting involved quite a bit of discussion, some disagreement, and concluded with the suggestion that each member of the faculty return an opinion form to the committee to indicate his or her interest in pursuing the subject further.

Fewer than 10% of the faculty expressed interest in further study; the vast majority wanted to maintain the status quo, some even asking, "Why did we even look at this topic?" This latter comment echoed a somewhat frustrating insight Mike had gained from the experience that year. Only one or two classroom teachers identified a problem that variable modular scheduling would resolve. Most indicated in no uncertain terms, "If it ain't broke, don't fix it!" That was 20 years ago; the school still has the same schedule.

This story suggests a few important points. First, solutions to undefined problems rarely succeed. When educators jump on passing bandwagons during each parade of hot, new trends, they seek change for the wrong reasons. As mentioned in an earlier chapter, they seek it primarily to impress others, usually parents and board members, or to grope randomly for ideas that seem to have merit.

Second, the principal in the story realized his inability to influence the faculty to accept change. The decisional processes in his school had been highly centralized, and, for years, he had imposed a range of new ideas on the faculty with little input from them. In the process, he had alienated progressively larger segments of the faculty, until, finally, he had alienated all of them. He knew that this initial attempt at a less centralized format needed the leadership of someone else if the concept was to have a chance in the building.

Third, without preliminary input from the faculty, they fail "to own" potential changes in the school's program. Furthermore, without their collaborative involvement throughout the change process, future solutions may fail to reflect the real needs of students and staff and rarely receive the support needed to make them work. Important ideas, then, though well-researched and conceptually sound, are denied a fighting chance in many of the nation's schools because they are applied to poorly defined problems or fail to receive the support of teachers and others with an investment in the instructional process.

TAKING ANOTHER LOOK AT EDUCATION'S TRENDS

Twenty years ago, variable modular scheduling was the star attraction in education's cavalcade of promising new ideas. Schools across the country explored the concept; a few implemented it. Some still use it. But like all trends, it enjoyed its brief appearance on the stage and then exited into obscurity. Its talent for publicity, however, is undeniable, so it has reappeared, this time with a new name—block scheduling.

So it is with all good trends. They appear, escorted by the finest names in education and promising to promote the changes that education requires to meet the constantly evolving needs of students. Then they disappear, only to be escorted out of obscurity 20 years later by the newest names in education, once again promising substantive change in schools across the country.

Consider some examples. Twenty years ago, the year-round school was receiving widespread attention. Today, it has reappeared, using the same name. Twenty years ago, educational journals were promoting the advantages of participative leadership. Today, they are emphasizing collaborative and transformational leadership, each a more convincing representative of improved leadership technique but dressed in fundamentally the same clothing.

Twenty years ago, educators talked about decentralization. Today, we are talking about site-based management. Twenty years ago, classes in educational *administration* were discussing facilitative and referent power. Today, classes in educational *leadership* are discussing the same thing. Twenty years ago, we wanted to reschool society. Today, we want to restructure schools. Twenty years ago, shared decision-making was challenging school hierarchies to promote broader decisional authority for teachers. Today, we seek "teacher empowerment." And so it goes.

Without substantive changes in our philosophical predispositions as administrators and in the planning activities we use to promote change, schools will continue to stand curbside as the parade of exciting and colorful new ideas marches into obscurity. Fortunately, we provide several exciting examples of how schools can accommodate such changes. Such changes avoid bandwagon acceptance of innovation and promote collaborative planning that resolves well-identified problems. Education's future, therefore, is not as bleak as some of us might expect.

WHAT IS THE FUTURE OF EDUCATION'S HIERARCHY?

First of all, it would appear that the hierarchy is here to stay. Hierarchically ordered relationships are as predictable in the nation's schools as they are on school playgrounds. Max Weber proposed his concepts of bureaucracy and hierarchy in the 1940s, and, in one form or another, they have prevailed in most of the nation's schools. They were not new at the time, having been evidenced in such specifics as Frederick Taylor's *Principles of Scientific Management* at the turn of the century and in the military chain of command centuries earlier.

Little in the literature suggests significant change in the hierarchical organization of schools. Much of the literature proposes decentralized and shared decision-making, transformational leadership, facilitative power, site-based management, collaborative planning, flatter organizational structures, and fewer bureaucratic interferences, but even the most enthusiastic cries for "restructuring" acknowledge that, whatever changes take place, it is likely to occur within the framework of hierarchical organization.

Given such sweeping concessions to the predominance of the hierarchy, cries to the contrary are particularly noteworthy. Consider the position of Donal Sacken, a professor of educational foundations at Texas Christian University. Sacken suggests that public education at the elementary, junior high, and secondary levels follow the example of universities by rotating administrative responsibilities among teachers, that current concepts of administration at the building level be virtually eliminated.

Part of his reasoning involves the apparent paradox that "prospective administrators spend time learning to lead people who often know more than the administrators themselves about the core organizational processes." Sacken apparently agrees with our earlier position, one that echoes throughout decades of administrative theorizing, that teachers know more about teaching than administrators.

Says Sacken about this inconsistency: "I basically agree with the teachers' argument that, to know teaching and to know students, you must teach. To designate as an evaluator of teaching someone who once taught but has now chosen to avoid it is offensive." "Offensive" it may be; it is certainly presumptuous, and it fails to promote the significant synergistic strength of teachers helping teachers.

We would agree with Sacken that graduate coursework for anyone seeking administrative certification, aside from a few foundations courses, rarely promotes a comprehensive understanding of the teaching/learning process. Administrative/leadership study normally involves budgetary considerations, legal issues, supervision, community relations, organizational decision-making, and such specifics as Total Quality Management.

Teachers, on the other hand, engage in postgraduate programs that emphasize learning theory, higher order thought process, classroom management, and such specifics as authentic assessment and modality learning. The gulf separating such areas of study for teachers and administrators seems to be widening, highlighting the inconsistencies inherent in "administrative evaluation" of teacher performance.

An outgrowth of such an inconsistency is administrative dependence on positional authority when evaluating teachers and a deemphasis on the expert power they gain from coursework and the accumulated knowledge of their own classroom experiences. Sacken's alternatives involve an administrative framework in schools that is composed of teachers on a rotating basis and revised university programs that deemphasize management theory and promote a better understanding of teaching and learning.

CAN IT HAPPEN?

Sacken's concepts have provoked serious thought and more than a little friendly disagreement in the Halls of Ivy. Some university personnel perceive them as being impractical, if conceptually desirable. They may agree with Sacken that the school principal is less the school's "educational leader" and more "the leader of educational leaders," but they recognize, as well, the tyranny of time and the purported inability of professionals to teach and administer simultaneously.

Yet, Sacken's ideas are being practiced in varying schools across the country. Consider these examples:

♦ The Cyrus Magnet School—The town of Cyrus, Minnesota, boasts a total population of 500 but has received national recognition for its innovative approach to school organization. Because of a declining enrollment, Cyrus was faced with closing its elementary and secondary schools or combining them into one, very different school. They decided to design a magnet school that would emphasize math, science, and technology and that would replace the old elementary school.

It was organized administratively along traditional lines, but budgetary restrictions soon resulted in the principal's resignation. The teachers took over. Says one of the teachers: "It leaves us money for other things, like state-of-the-art technology. People who visit our school can't believe how hard we work. But making our own decisions energizes us and makes us feel connected to everything we do. We can be as creative as we need to be."

♦ La Escuela Fratney—La Escuela Fratney is located in Milwaukee, Wisconsin, and is composed of mostly African-American and Latino children. When the school board had decided to turn the community's school into a professional development school, teachers and parents proposed an alternative that would emphasize two-way bilingual instruction, multiculturalism, whole language, and cooperative learning. They also proposed to run the school without an "administrative staff."

The school has been operational for several years and has resulted in significant learning experiences for the staff as well as the students. Regarding the operation of the school without a principal, said one of the teachers: "We had to learn everything from how to read a school budget to the science of ordering office supplies to the red tape involved in school renovations." The experience nonetheless had its advantages.

Said another teacher: ". . . We, as teachers, are challenged to use our creativity to its fullest. That's not something we could have done if things had stayed the same, or if we worked in a more traditional setting." The comment is particularly appropriate as a summary for this book. "A more traditional setting" and the need to modify it with the collaborative involvement of teachers, students, and parents is our focus. It can be realized by schools with a common vision of organizational purpose and the courage to break ranks and escape the lockstep of tradition.

♦ Sweeney Elementary—Located in Santa Fe, New Mexico, Sweeney Elementary is one such school. When the school principal left to assume a state-level position, the teachers requested that the board of education give them administrative authority and obviate the need for a new principal. The board balked at their initial request but, in the end, agreed to accept their proposal for one school year, primarily because of the support of parents and the rest of the community.

Today, the school is managed by a four-teacher team, which is elected every 2 years. Teachers also serve on a variety of committees. The time commitment is significant. Said one teacher of her administrative responsibilities: "When the staff nominated me for this job, I had to do some real soul-searching. I'm an old-fashioned teacher, a paper-grader. How much time would this take away from my class?" But another teacher responded: "After being in very traditional classrooms, marching the straight and narrow and not interacting very much with each other, this is a new awakening."

A NEW AWAKENING

To what extent is this new awakening reflected in the thinking of administrators and teachers in traditional schools? To answer this question, we surveyed 30 superintendents and 30 teachers from a Midwestern state. The responses may vary somewhat from the perceptions of teachers and administrators in other states, but they provide interesting insights into the likely future of collaboration in the nation's schools.

Regarding the future of collaboration in schools, 26 of the 30 superintendents indicated that teachers will increase their participation in administrative decision-making moderately to significantly. Of the few superintendents who disagreed, two felt that teachers have become apathetic, and one indicated that most teachers are really not that interested in collaborative activity, especially regarding decision-making.

Another superintendent expressed a similar position by indicating that there's "too much heat in the kitchen" for teachers. He indicated that when given the opportunity to participate, many teachers find the time consumption too great to continue. Their involvement either detracts from their effectiveness in the classroom or provokes a total time commitment that too many teachers are unwilling to make.

Most of the superintendents felt strongly about the need for teacher participation on an input basis. Superintendents and boards of education across the country have developed advisory committees composed of elected teacher representatives to provide input into district decision-making. Although such teachers rarely make terminal decisions regarding such issues or have little opportunity to discuss or argue salient points, they are expected to dialogue with central office personnel and board members regarding district policies, salary, and other employment considerations.

Again, Senge's distinction between discussion and dialogue helps clarify the nature of collaborative activity in schools. According to most of the superintendents in our survey, collaboration among school personnel emphasizes dialogue, the nonjudgmental sharing of individual thought and the collective exploration of new ideas. It emphasizes inquiry instead of analysis and reflection instead of actual decision-making.

Most of the superintendents felt that the administrative team approach would promote more dialogue among administrators and teachers. The teachers we surveyed, however, were less inclined to agree. One teacher indicated that hierarchically ordered relationships interfere with purposeful communication between teachers and administrators, that such relationships presuppose positions of superiority for administrators and inferiority for teachers.

Some administrators may consider such a comment an isolated example of one teacher's frustration. The increasing demands of teachers for collaborative activity in schools, however, a characteristic affirmed by Sacken earlier in this chapter, seems to reflect a need for professional parity within schools. This area of relative status positions requires further study, as it seems to have significance for the whole question of collaboration.

Finally, we asked both groups if the large supply of teachers would make them more passive during their interactions with administrators. Both the superintendents and the teachers indicated that this was very unlikely. The teachers, however, made some very pointed comments. One commented that the time seems right for increased involvement in decision-making. He doubted, however, that teachers would ever be provided with sufficient information to make helpful decisions.

Another indicated that teachers, more so than administrators, are more in tune with what is going on in the school. On that basis, she felt that ongoing collaboration promoted not only teacher ownership of school decisions but more substantive dialogue of student and teacher needs. A third teacher indicated that classroom teaching is more demanding and less personally fulfilling than ever before, that the gap between administrators and teachers interferes with ongoing planning activity and the development of mutually appropriate support networks.

A fourth felt that schools are top-heavy with administrators and that many teachers blame current frustrations on the inability or the reluctance of some administrators to act. Several teachers felt that, even if given the opportunity for increased collaboration, many teachers eventually would refuse to participate. This observation is significant. It suggests that any plan to improve school collaboration must recognize that the teacher's primary responsibility is to his or her students.

Such a responsibility involves substantial time, especially in light of ever-emerging methodologies and technologies. Without some organizational redesign, many plans for improved school collaboration will fail. And those that function partially may do so without ever resolving the problems affecting teacher dissatisfaction or ineffective organizational planning.

TAKING A LOOK AT THE CURRENT LITERATURE

Marsick and Watkins indicated in a recent edition of *Resource Development Quarterly* that current barriers to effective schools include the inability of many educators to change mental models, to avoid learned helplessness, to modify cultures of disrespect and fear, to revitalize an entrenched bureaucracy, and to overcome the limitations of a part-time workforce.

Similarly, Smith and Meier, in the *Public Administration Review*, suggest problems with bureaucratic organization but affirm it as education's current best way to accommodate administration. They suggest that reducing bureaucracy will burden teachers with administrative tasks and harm their performance rather than improve it. This has been a recurring concern during our discussions with university personnel and practicing administrators and teachers.

Goldman, et al., in a paper presented at the annual meeting of the American Educational Research Association, indicate that relevant change is possible in schools if the following conditions apply: a ready staff, a supportive principal, a shared vision, and a minimum of bureaucratic interference. They also expressed the need for more precise definitions of "restructuring" and "site-based management," better descriptions of the actual restructuring process in schools, and more discussion of altered uses of power in schools and how it influences the attitudes and behaviors of teachers and administrators.

This question of power and its relationship to teacher and administrator behavior is significant. "Power sharing" and "teacher empowerment" are recurring trends in the literature. Dunlap and Goldman, in their booklet *"Facilitative" Power in Special Education and Clinical Supervision*, for example, argue that facilitative power is the best alternative to hierarchical or positional power. They indicate further that facilitative power is becoming increasingly common in schools where administrators are willing to modify decision-making to accommodate expert power and collegial cooperation. These administrators have discovered that facilitative power encourages innovative approaches to planning and problem-solving and highlights the limitations of traditional power concepts.

It is important to observe that much of the literature discusses the sharing of power and the importance of dialogue within "restructured" organizations. With the exception of writers like Sacken, et al., most writers are assuming, even encouraging, the continuation of hierarchical organization within the modification of the present school system. The future of the educational hierarchy, therefore, seems assured. For collaboration to occur, however, administrators must acknowledge a couple additional points.

THE MOST LIKELY FUTURE

The hierarchy will remain. It may be flatter and more user-friendly, but schools, like most organizations, will continue to gradate levels of authority and responsibility. Within that framework, however, the literature assures us, and we tend to agree, that schools will continue to seek increased collaboration. Call it shared decision-making, site-based management, or teacher empowerment, collaboration will remain desirable conceptually, if not always functionally.

Its functionality relates less to its desirability than to the skills of those seeking to use it. If facilitative power is to replace positional or hierarchical power and promote increased collaboration in schools, the behaviors of administrators as well as teachers will require significant change. It is not enough for educators to accept the need for a shared vision within the school or to believe in the value of collegial supervision, teacher empowerment, or facilitative power.

What is needed is that administrator and teacher *behaviors* reflect these changed attitudes and values. In essence, how do administrators *behave* when they are seeking a shared vision within the school? How do teachers *behave* when they are interacting collaboratively with administrators and other teachers? How does facilitative power become *reality* in school's that express a belief in collaboration? Finally, and most importantly, how do administrators *behave* when they empower teachers?

Committing conceptually to teacher empowerment and collaborative activity in the school is not enough. Discussing them in the school and throughout the community as personal and professional goals is not enough. Administrators must reflect in their daily behavior a willingness to seek and value the ideas of teachers, parents, and students and to devise processes that routinely seek such ideas. Integrating such behaviors is more difficult than most of us realize.

Most young administrators, particularly those helped up the hierarchy by veteran colleagues, have been conditioned only incidentally by occasional leadership courses in local universities. Most of their thinking and behavior are shaped by daily interactions within the school culture. In essence, their behavior is influenced not so much by distant theoretical principles but by immediate daily contact with traditionally accepted notions of administrative behavior.

Only a relatively few educators seem willing to scale the steep slopes of education's hierarchy to become administrators. Some seek administration because of its elevated position and improved salary, others for its expanded view of the school. Many find both. Their climb is rewarded with broadened opportunities to reach into the personal and professional lives of students and teachers. Some try to use these opportunities to collaborate with teachers and to empower them.

Others scale administration's slopes only to find isolation at the top. The behaviors they choose to reflect their philosophies create walls instead of bridges. They fail to realize that their own needs within the school are inextricably bound to the needs of others, particularly to their teaching colleagues. This failure often results in a curious loss of power and the unexplained inability to influence school programs and teacher behaviors.

Even the many administrators who seek to empower teachers lose sight of the fact that teachers, in one important respect, are already "empowered." They may not have the power they want to change the curriculum, improve their supervisory responsibilities, or develop the teaching schedules they want, but they do have the power to *allow* administrators to effect change in school programs as well as in their own teaching and personal behaviors. Such power is not theirs to use, but to give.

To acknowledge, then, that teachers empower administrators is to accept a subtle reality rooted in the daily interactions of school personnel. Power, therefore, flows two ways. That much of the professional literature seeks to empower teachers is consistent with current notions of shared decision-making and site-based management. Collaboration in schools may not include terminal decision-making authorities for teachers, but it will promote the kind of dialogue that results in needed change.

That collaboration also empowers administrators is a fact overlooked in much of the literature. Hopefully, the programs and the concepts we have presented in this book will enable more schools to realize that everyone in the system benefits from collaborative activity, especially the students, who realize substantive improvements in their educational experiences.

SELECTED BIBLIOGRAPHY

Barker, Joel Arthur. *Future Edge: Discovering the New Paradigms of Success.* New York: William Morrow & Co., 1992.

Bennis, Warren, and Nanus, Burt. *Leaders: The Strategies for Taking Charge.* NewYork: Harper & Row, 1985.

Block, Peter. *The Empowered Manager.* San Francisco: Jossey-Bass, 1987.

Bolman, Lee G., and Deal, Terrence E. *Leading With Soul: An Uncommon Journey of Spirit.* San Francisco: Jossey-Bass, 1995.

Byham, William C. *Zapp! In Education.* New York: Fawcett Columbine, 1992.

Byrnes, Margaret A., and Cornesky, Robert A. *Quality Fusion: Turning Total Quality Management into Classroom Practice.* Port Orange, FL: Cornesky & Assoc. Press, 1994.

Byrnes, Margaret A., Cornesky, Robert A., and Byrnes, Lawrence W. *The Quality Teacher: Implementing Total Quality Management in the Classroom.* Port Orange, FL: Cornesky & Assoc. Press, 1995.

Covey, Stephen R. *Principle-Centered Leadership.* New York: Summit Books, 1990.

Covey, Stephen R. *The Seven Habits of Highly Effective People: Restating the Character Ethic.* Simon & Schuster, 1989.

Deal, Terrence, and Peterson, Kent. *The Leadership Paradox.* San Francisco: Jossey-Bass, 1994.

Deming, W. Edwards. *Out of the Crisis,* 2nd Edition. Cambridge, MA: MIT Center for Advanced Engineering Study, 1986.

Deming, W. Edwards. *The New Economics for Industry, Government, Education.* Cambridge, MA: MIT Center for Advanced Engineering Study, 1993.

Dobyns, Lloyd, and Crawford-Mason, Clare. *Thinking About Quality: Progress, Wisdom and the Deming Philosophy*. New York: Times Books/Random House, 1994.

Drucker, Peter F. *Managing for the Future: The 1990's and Beyond*. New York: Truman Talley Books/Dutton, 1992.

Glasser, William M. *The Quality School*. New York: Harper & Row, 1990.

Glasser, William M. *The Quality School Teacher: A Companion Volume to the Quality School*. New York: Perennial Library, Harper & Row, 1993.

Imai, Masaaki. *Kaizen: The Key To Japan's Competitive Success*. New York: McGraw Hill, 1986.

Kearns, David T., and Doyle, Denis P. *Winning the Brain Race: A Bold Plan to Make Our Schools Competitive*. Institute for Contemporary Studies, 1989.

Kozol, Jonathan. *Savage Inequalities: Children in America's Schools*. New York: Crown Publishers, 1991.

Lundy, James L. *TEAMS (Together Each Achieves More Success): How to Develop Peak Performance Teams for World-Class Results*. Chicago: Dartnell, 1994.

McCormick, Betty L. *Quality and Education: Critical Linkages*. Princeton Junction, NJ: Eye on Education, 1993.

Peters, Tom, and Waterman, Jr., Robert H. *In Search of Excellence*. New York : Warner Books, 1982.

Schargel, Franklin. *Transforming Education Through Total Quality Management: A Practitioner's Guide*. Princeton Junction, NJ: Eye on Education, 1994.

Senge, Peter M. *The Fifth Discipline: The Art and Practice of the Learning Organization*. New York: Doubleday/Currency, 1990.

#0207 - 170717 - C0 - 229/152/12 - PB - 9781883001308